Already published in the series (*continued*):

F. SCOTT FITZGERALD: THE GREAT GATSBY

by

JOHN S. WHITLEY

Lecturer in English and American Literature,
University of Sussex

EDWARD ARNOLD

© JOHN S. WHITLEY 1976

First published 1976
by Edward Arnold (Publishers) Ltd,
41 Bedford Square, London WC1B 3DQ

Reprinted 1980, 1984

ISBN ~~0 7131 5873 5~~

0413158724

For Lin

Printed and bound in Great Britain at
The Camelot Press Ltd, Southampton

General Preface

The object of this series is to provide studies of individual novels, plays and groups of poems and essays which are known to be widely read by students. The emphasis is on clarification and evaluation; biographical and historical facts, while they may be discussed when they throw light on particular elements in a writer's work, are generally subordinated to critical discussion. What kind of work is this? What exactly goes on here? How good is this work, and why? These are the questions that each writer will try to answer.

It should be emphasized that these studies are written on the assumption that the reader has already read carefully the work discussed. The objective is not to enable students to deliver opinions about works they have not read, nor is it to provide ready-made ideas to be applied to works that have been read. In one sense all critical interpretation can be regarded as foisting opinions on readers, but to accept this is to deny the advantages of any sort of critical discussion directed at students or indeed at anybody else. The aim of these studies is to provide what Coleridge called in another context 'aids to reflection' about the works discussed. The interpretations are offered as suggestive rather than as definitive, in the hope of stimulating the reader into developing further his own insights. This is after all the function of all critical discourse among sensible people.

Because of the interest which this kind of study has aroused, it has been decided to extend it first from merely English literature to include also some selected works of American literature and now further to include selected works in English by Commonwealth writers. The criterion will remain that the book studied is important in itself and is widely read by students.

DAVID DAICHES

Contents

Note: The bibliography gives the original date of publication of each work. The dates given in the footnotes are those of the editions consulted and need not be those of the original editions.

Page numbers in parenthesis after a quotation refer to the Penguin editions of the following frequently-cited texts:

Joseph Conrad, *Heart of Darkness* (1975)
F. Scott Fitzgerald, *Bernice Bobs Her Hair* (1974)
    The Crack-Up (1974)
    The Great Gatsby (1974)
Herman Melville, *Moby-Dick* (1975)
Andrew Turnbull (ed.), *The Letters of F. Scott Fitzgerald* (1968)

1 Introduction

A dream is not a very safe thing to be near. . . . It's like a loaded pistol with a hair trigger; if it stays alive long enough, somebody is going to be hurt. But if it's a good dream, it's worth it. There are not many dreams in the world, but there are a lot of human lives.

William Faulkner, in *The Unvanquished* (1938)

F. Scott Fitzgerald is particularly known as an *American* writer, not merely because he was born in America and lived most of his life there, nor because he wrote about that country and its inhabitants, but because, with his second collection of stories, *Tales of the Jazz Age* (1922), he gave the most enduring name to the 1920s in America and captured more vividly than any of his contemporary writers the mood and mores of these confused and confusing years. He is a writer noted for his treatment of 'the American Dream' and for the vividness with which he places his characters within a continuity of American history. Of course, his greatest single achievement, *The Great Gatsby* (1925), contains many illuminations and criticisms of American life following the end of the First World War. The 'Americanness' of the novel is emphasized by such thematic considerations as the move from West to East; the relationship of Gatsby's material achievements to the Benjamin Franklin/Horatio Alger myth of 'rags to riches'; the tremendous growth of the automobile industry; the poverty of spiritual life in America during her most hedonistic decade and the marvel and futility of that persistent search for the numinous which has always characterized the progress of the American imagination. Finally, as Arthur Mizener has pointed out:

'Let me tell you about the very rich' he began in one of his finest stories; and with the establishment of this dramatically balanced view of the rich in *The Great Gatsby* he had found his theme and his fable, for wealth was Fitzgerald's central symbol; around it he eventually built a mythology which enabled him to take imaginative possession of American life.[1]

I have in no way wished to minimize the importance of these aspects of *The Great Gatsby* and, indeed, I have tried to explicate them as fully as the confines of such a brief study would allow. However, I have also tried to widen the range of references to articulate my view that Fitzgerald's novel is a great world novel and that it can exert a tremendous effect on readers whose awareness of American history and culture is minimal. As one American poet, Longfellow, said:

> All that is best in the great poets of all countries is not what is national in them, but what is universal. Their roots are in their native soil; but their branches wave in the unpatriotic air, that speaks the same language unto all men, and their leaves shine with the illimitable light that pervades all lands.[2]

I have tried to stress this universal appeal by placing Fitzgerald in a context of various writers, both European and American. I have placed considerable emphasis on two non-American writers who have clearly influenced his work, John Keats and Joseph Conrad. The question of literary influence is, of course, difficult and nebulous. That Fitzgerald knew and loved the work of both writers is clear from a reading of his letters, but I do not mean to suggest that he wrote his novel with their works constantly at his elbow, nor that he could not have written the novel without knowing about them. Nevertheless, in writing about a man who tried to make over the real world in his image of beauty and truth he naturally turned to a poet who celebrated the emotional, imaginative response of the individual mind, the subjection of reason to the verity of imaginative apprehension. He required, however, that a balanced view be taken of such a hero, a view which tried to balance the Romantic values against the needs of man as a social creature, a view which could appreciate while remaining reasonably objective. Hence he took, from Conrad's *Lord Jim* (1900) and *Heart of Darkness* (1902), the 'middleman' narrator, Marlow, and turned him into that careful mid-

---

[1] Arthur Mizener, 'Scott Fitzgerald and the Imaginative Possession of American Life', *Sewanee Review* LIV (Winter, 1946), pp. 66–86. Taken from Morton Dauwen Zabel (ed.), *Literary Opinion in America*, vol. I (New York, 1962), p. xli.

[2] H. W. Longfellow, *Kavanagh* (New Haven, 1965), p. 86.

Westerner, Nick Carraway. Fitzgerald referred to Conrad's Preface to *The Nigger of the 'Narcissus'* (1897) as affording him 'the greatest "credo" in my life ever since I decided that I would rather be an artist than a careerist' (59), for it taught him that 'the most important thing about a work of fiction is that the essential reaction shall be profound and enduring' (382). The following is one of the most significant passages in Conrad's Preface:

> To snatch in a moment of courage, from the remorseless rush of time, a passing phase of life, is only the beginning of the task. The task approached in tenderness and faith is to hold up unquestioningly, without choice and without fear, the rescued fragment before all eyes in the light of a sincere mood. It is to show its vibration, its colour. its form; and through its movement, its form, and its colour, reveal the substance of its truth—disclose its inspiring secret: the stress and passion within the core of each convincing moment. In a single-minded attempt of that kind, if one be deserving and fortunate, one may perchance attain to such clearness of sincerity that at last the presented vision of regret or pity, of terror or mirth, shall awaken in the hearts of the beholders that feeling of unavoidable solidarity; of the solidarity in mysterious origin, in toil, in joy, in hope, in uncertain fate, which binds men to each other and all mankind to the visible world.

It is Nick Carraway's task to hold up such a rescued fragment as the story of Gatsby, to reveal the substance of its truth and, through his own reactions, to awaken in the hearts of his readers an astonished sense of our own solidarity, our empathy with the fate of a monomaniac millionaire bootlegger. In two of his most successful works, *Lord Jim* and *Heart of Darkness*, Conrad confronts us with similar charismatic and enigmatic characters, Jim and Kurtz. At one point in *Lord Jim*, Marlow looks at the title figure silhouetted against the night sea:

> For me the white figure in the stillness of coast and sea seemed to stand at the heart of a vast enigma.[3]

This description is closely paralleled by Nick's first sight of Gatsby. It was necessary for Conrad to find a mode of narration which would make clear the subtle balance of attraction/repulsion which such enigmatic

[3] Robert Emmet Long, '*The Great Gatsby* and the Tradition of Joseph Conrad: Part I', *Texas Studies in Literature and Language* VIII, no. 2 (Summer, 1966), p. 275.

figures would arouse in those who came across them. For this purpose
the detached narrative objectivity of Flaubert, though Conrad much
admired it, was inadequate. As Albert Guerard puts it:

> The critical struggle, technically speaking, was to discover a narrator
> nominally not the author himself, not committed to consecutive
> reporting, and who could move where he wished in time, space and
> thought.[4]

Shortly after the publication of *Gatsby*, Fitzgerald wrote a reply to H. L.
Mencken's criticism that 'the story is fundamentally trivial' and asserted:

> Despite your admiration of Conrad you have lately—perhaps in
> reaction against the merely well made novels of James'
> imitators—become used to the formless. It is in protest against my own
> formless two novels, and Lewis' and Dos Passos' that this was written
> (500).

The most important aspect of *Gatsby* as a 'constructed novel' is clearly the
use of a first-person narrator recalling events in the past.
  From the preceding comments it must follow that I regard Gatsby and
his dream as serious and important and that I believe Nick Carraway to
be a reliable narrator. As well as Mencken, Marjorie Kinnan Rawlings
felt that Fitzgerald wrote about 'trivial people' (266) and more recent
critics have echoed this. As late as 1971 C. W. E. Bigsby could write:

> But surely the defeat of Gatsby finally signifies little but the demise of
> a kind of futile romanticism which had little to recommend it
> anyway.[5]

Such a view can only be obtained by abstracting Gatsby from the context
within which we are asked to view him. No doubt most of the great
charismatic figures of literature, Don Quixote, Ahab, Thomas Sutpen,
would, as Albert Guerard has pointed out, prove tiresome if not
impossible companions in real life. But, as Guerard says:

> Art induces greater sympathies (but also sterner judgments) than most
> of us are capable of in the daily conduct of our lives.[6]

[4] Albert Guerard, *Conrad the Novelist* (Cambridge, Mass., 1958), p. 62.
[5] C. W. E. Bigsby, 'The Two Identities of F. Scott Fitzgerald'. In Malcolm
Bradbury and David Palmer (eds), *The American Novel and the Nineteen Twenties*
(London, 1971), p. 137.   [6] *Conrad the Novelist, op. cit.*, p. 129.

ence. If, as one recent dictionary of literary terms suggests, the he[ro of a] work is simply the most important character in that work[10] then [it woul]d be difficult not to accord Gatsby that status; but if, as many read[ers migh]t feel, the hero is one who has a discernible growth a[nd dev]elopment to a point of some kind of recognition, then *The Gr[eat Ga]tsby* must finally be seen as Nick Carraway's story.

[10] Karl Beckson and Arthur Ganz, *A Reader's Guide to Literary Terms* (Ne[w Y]ork, 1960), p. 72.

Gatsby's tragedy cannot be viewed in the light of such commonsensical levelling as Bigsby's since it is consistently filtered to us through the eyes of Nick, eyes which strive to see as fully 'round' Gatsby as possible and by doing so create a fruitful ambivalence, a tension between hope and despair which totally engages the sympathies of the reader and prevents any simple adulation or dismissal.

Of course, the anti-levelling point of view assumes that Nick is a reliable narrator, that is to say one whom we believe to be setting down an honest and accurate account of events and one whose account is not compromised by any other view we are invited to take. In this respect, he differs from Nelly Dean, for example, the narrator in *Wuthering Heights* (1847). Nelly is honest and tells the truth as she sees it but the combination of an objective view of her character (by Lockwood), the circumstances of her narration (a sick-bed gossip to cheer Lockwood) and the brilliant manner in which Emily Brontë allows Nelly's character to emerge from her relentlessly practical and smug north-country language encourages us to be wary of her judgments and to look beyond them to try and find our own. No such distance between narrator and reader occurs in *The Great Gatsby*. Our knowledge of Gatsby's story is always coexistent with our knowledge of the narrator.

The case against Nick was most trenchantly made twenty years ago by R. W. Stallman. Insisting that 'the moral rectitude of Nick is but a mask of hypocrisy', Stallman characterizes Carraway as a 'defunct arch-priest' and a 'prig' who belongs irredeemably to the West, 'the land of the unliving', because his main aim is to 'police' the world 'morally', an aim which negates faith in humanity and 'marks his own spiritual bankruptcy'.[7] Stallman's essay on *The Great Gatsby* is full of brilliant insights but his judgment of Nick seems one-sided, to say the least. His basic mistake, perhaps, is to assume that for Nick to be reliable he must be wholly sympathetic. No such necessity exists. When Nick breaks off his relationship with Jordan she clearly feels badly treated. In a way she *has* been badly treated and Nick's narrative accepts this:

> There was one thing to be done before I left, an awkward, unpleasant thing that perhaps had better have been let alone. But I wanted to leave

[7] R. W. Stallman, 'Gatsby and the Hole in Time', *Modern Fiction Studies* I, no. 4 (November, 1955). Reprinted in R. W. Stallman, *The Houses that James Built* (East Lansing, 1961), pp. 135–7.

things in order and not just trust that obliging and indifferent sea to sweep my refuse away (184).

This can easily sound priggish but only if abstracted from its context. Nick's journey East has shown him much carelessness; either the squalid carelessness of the Buchanans or the splendid but wasteful Romanticism of Gatsby. By the fact of telling the story in retrospect he clearly admits his partial corruption by the East, his treatment of Jordan, his role as a pander, his temporary abandonment of that mid-Western morality associated with 'real snow' and the 'sharp wild brace' (182) of the Wisconsin night air; but he just as clearly shows us his recognition of that moral carelessness and a wish to return to his moral roots, however limited such a move might be. He is never as assertively dogmatic as Stallman suggests. His statement that,

> When I came back from the East last autumn I felt that I wanted the world to be in uniform and at a sort of moral attention forever; I wanted no more riotous excursions with privileged glimpses into the human heart. (8)

is surely a psychologically realistic result after all he has been through and does not, cannot, negate the complexities of Nick's awareness of Gatsby's story.

Our feelings about Nick's dismissal of Jordan may be related to our response to Prince Hal in Shakespeare's *Henry IV* Part I. Hal's treatment of Falstaff and the other low-life characters (and, to some extent, Hotspur) may be seen as 'priggish' and 'hypocritical' and there are times at which, like Nick, he seems cold and neutral when placed against the richness of the charismatic characters. Yet he does represent order in a potentially chaotic world and so remains the closest point of reference for the audience. Shakespeare's order, vested in kingship, is far more certainly emphasized than Fitzgerald's but we can say that Nick is the only character who feels, however tentatively, that there must be some larger reason for living than the dictates of the self. Fitzgerald, as a lapsed Catholic, seemed to feel that himself; in his 1934 introduction to the Modern Library edition of his novel he wrote:

> How anyone could take up the responsibility of being a novelist without a sharp and concise attitude to life is a puzzle to me.[8]

[8] Quoted in Frederick J. Hoffman (ed.), *'The Great Gatsby': a Study* (New York, 1962), p. 166.

That attitude, if it exists in *The Great* ... Carraway. Gatsby, like Ahab and Thoma... according to a grand design and so he, like th... change or development. For all his 'greatness' h... introduces himself as a man 'inclined to reserve a... insists that this attitude has laid him open to cont... strange people. He reminds us here of Marlow at... chapter 5 of *Lord Jim*, who is similarly a prey to

> ... the kind of thing that by devious, unexpected, tr... ways causes me to run up against men with soft spots, wit... with hidden plague spots, by Jove! and loosens their tong... sight of me for their infernal confidences ...

Yet Nick immediately qualifies this 'openness' by adding th... tolerance has a limit:

> Conduct may be founded on the hard rock or the wet marshes, b... after a certain point I don't care what it's founded on (7–8).

By this important qualification, as Thomas Hanzo points out,

> ... Nick insists that action reveals some principle and that toleration does not permit indifference.[9]

and from then on it is possible to trace a kind of learning process in Nick's involvement with Gatsby, not so much in what he does as in the selection and arrangements of his materials for telling the story. We cannot judge Nick's treatment of Jordan without seeing it as a parallel to the Gatsby/Daisy relationship nor can we interpret the references to driving in their final meeting without placing these references within the morally-directed range of automobile metaphors throughout the novel. We cannot interpret Nick's reaction to Gatsby's party in chapter 3 without relating this to his views of the parties in chapter 2 and chapter 6 nor can we understand the importance of Jimmy Gatz's SCHEDULE in chapter 9 without placing it in the context of the Horatio Alger-like 'American dream' which reflects not merely on Gatsby's 'progress' but on Nick's also. By the methods he uses to tell his story Nick shows us his development. His way of ordering his experiences involves his view of

[9] Thomas Hanzo, 'The Theme and Narrator of *The Great Gatsby*', *Modern Fiction Studies* II (Winter, 1956–7), pp. 183–90. Reprinted in Hoffman, *op. cit.*, p. 289.

experie... of a w... would... might... dev... G...

2 Gatsby

One of Fitzgerald's favourite writers was the Romantic poet, John Keats. Keats is mentioned numerous times in Fitzgerald's letters. Writing to his daughter, Scottie, in 1940, he said:

> 'The Grecian Urn' is unbearably beautiful with every syllable as inevitable as the notes in Beethoven's Ninth Symphony or it's just something you don't understand. It is what it is because an extraordinary genius paused at that point in history and touched it. I suppose I've read it a hundred times. About the tenth time I began to know what it was about, and caught the chime in it and the exquisite inner mechanics. Likewise with 'The Nightingale' which I can never read through without tears in my eyes; likewise the 'Pot of Basil' with its great stanzas about the two brothers, 'Why were they proud, etc.'; and 'The Eve of St. Agnes', which has the richest, most sensuous imagery in English, not excepting Shakespeare. And finally his three or four great sonnets, 'Bright Star' and the others (104).

Sheila Graham in *College of One* mentions the novelist, at an early stage in their relationship, 'quoting from his beloved Keats'[1] and she notes that, 'at Princeton he had decided he would write prose on the same fine lines as Keats's poetry'.[2] The title of one of his novels, *Tender is the Night*, is drawn directly from Keats and *The Great Gatsby* contains at least three obvious memories of 'Ode to a Nightingale'. The first occurs during Nick's initial meeting with the Buchanans on East Egg:

> 'I looked outdoors for a minute, and it's very romantic outdoors. There's a bird on the lawn that I think must be a nightingale come over on the Cunard or White Star Line. He's singing away.' (22)

the second near the end of chapter 5:

[1] Sheila Graham, *College of One* (Harmondsworth, 1969), p. 71.
[2] *ibid.*, p. 95.

He lit Daisy's cigarette from a trembling match, and sat down with her on a couch far across the room, where there was no light save what the gleaming floor bounced in from the hall. (102)

and the third just after that when Nick is attempting to analyse Daisy's effect on Gatsby:

I think that voice held him most, with its fluctuating, feverish warmth, because it couldn't be over-dreamed—that voice was a deathless song (103).

The 'deathless' quality of her voice corresponds to that of Keats's nightingale: 'Thou wast not born for death, immortal Bird!'

Of course, since Keats was one of Fitzgerald's favourite writers, the discovery of such debts is hardly unexpected and may serve as no more than an amusing piece of literary detective work. However, Keats's influence on Fitzgerald seems much more profound than mere illustrative 'borrowing' and may be followed in an attempt to explain just why the term 'Romantic' is appropriate to the figure of Gatsby. As Richard D. Lehan remarks, 'Time is the real enemy in the Romantic world',[3] and Keats is constantly striving to achieve a vision which will somehow defeat time, not by abandoning chronological sequence altogether but by working towards a fusion of process and immobility which will transcend the normally destructive operations of time and its attendant lords, disillusion and mortality. The problem is clearly shown, though not solved, in 'Ode on a Grecian Urn'. Here the Grecian artist has achieved a kind of perfection by freezing a moment into a work of art which appeals to the total imaginative apprehension rather than merely to one or several of the senses:

> Heard melodies are sweet, but those unheard
> Are sweeter; therefore, ye soft pipes, play on;
> Not to the sensual ear, but, more endear'd,
> Pipe to the spirit ditties of no tone.

The work of art is permanent; the world of which the poet is a part is mortal and so temporary, a world of 'a burning forehead, and a parching tongue'. In stanza 4 the poet addresses questions to the static work of art, questions emanating from the world of process. These highlight the

---

[3] Richard D. Lehan, *F. Scott Fitzgerald and the Craft of Fiction* (Carbondale and Edwardsville, 1966), p. 5.

inhumanity of the static work, the fact that only by being totally removed from the world of disillusion and death can that work survive and by surviving it becomes 'cold' and heartless. A more successful coalescence of process and immobility can be seen in 'Ode to Autumn' where the season of autumn is accepted as a transitional period between summer and winter: the movement of time is emphasized (the day is 'soft-dying', the swallows are 'gathering') but often in such a way as to slow it down to a point where it comes very close to stopping ('the last oozings hours by hours'). The personifications of autumn combine movement and non-movement: a woman's hair is 'soft-lifted by the winnowing wind' while the rest of her body sits; the gleaner's legs carry her across the brook while her head is kept perfectly 'steady'. So Keats is able to combine a sense of prolonged fulfilment ('Until they think warm days will never cease') with a sense of the endless continuity of the seasonal cycle. The magnificent coalescence of time and the timeless has an obvious relationship with Keats's feeling, strongest towards the end of his life, that poets must be 'those to whom the miseries of the world / Are misery, and will not let them rest.' The true poet can see eternity only by being firmly rooted in the time-bound world of his fellow mortals whom he helps and who, in turn, offer comfort and support to his efforts. Diogenes Teufelsdrockh, the hero of Carlyle's *Sartor Resartus* (1833–4), comes to a similar conclusion:

> For man lives in Time, has his whole earthly being, endeavour and destiny shaped for him by Time: only in the transitory Time-Symbol is the ever-motionless Eternity we stand on made manifest.

As we shall see, Gatsby's Platonic view of himself can only exist in a timeless realm which is constantly made to seem very fragile when exposed to the other selves, including even Daisy, who surround Gatsby. For Gatsby there is no opportunity for coalescence (and hence no merging of 'I' and 'Thou'), only polarization and ultimate defeat.

Gatsby is a Romantic attempting to maintain a search for ideality in an era totally inimical to such a venture. The 1920s were characterized, both in their own time and since, as an age of excess. The war of 1914–18 had instigated a collapse of values and a corresponding search for pleasure. Prohibition forced much of that pleasure underground, causing an increase in its hedonistic voraciousness and sense of sin. With hindsight we can now see the ebullience of the period as more than a little desperate, covering economic disasters, appalling labour disputes,

the emergence of Gatsby → Fuller McGee case

insecure isolationism, a decline in religious faith with a corresponding display of cynicism and an unbalanced conservatism resulting, among other things, in increased activity by the Ku Klux Klan.

NB

Following the Great War, the myth of the self-made man, though still trumpeted proudly by the advertising executives, was beginning to acquire a somewhat tarnished look. One of Fitzgerald's ideas for Gatsby came from his knowledge of the Fuller-McGee case. Edward M. Fuller had been a neighbour of the Fitzgeralds in Great Neck, Long Island, two years before *Gatsby* was published. Fuller and McGee were prosecuted for illegal speculation with their customers' money and it was discovered that the 'brains' behind these transactions was Arnold Rothstein, a well-known gangster who had fixed the baseball World Series of 1919. Just as Meyer Wolfsheim is based on Rothstein, so Gatsby is based on Fuller, at least to the extent of his relationship with Wolfsheim. That Gatsby has made a great deal of money from various kinds of illegal speculation is made clear from the phone-call which comes after his death:

> 'Young Parker's in trouble', he said rapidly. 'They picked him up when he handed the bonds over the counter.' (173)

NB

AIM OF FFS. TBS FORD

Fitzgerald wished to follow the example of Sinclair Lewis's *Babbitt* (1922) in showing the moral vacuum towards which America was heading in her ever-increasing concern with measuring her heroes in terms of their material success. Fitzgerald moves at least one step beyond Lewis, of course, in making the materialist and the artist who must deny materialism coexist in one person.

Hand in hand with all this went the materialist boom spearheaded by the figure of Henry Ford. In his terrifying novel, *Journey to the End of the Night* (1932), Louis Ferdinand Céline drew on his experiences at Ford's River Rouge plant in Dearborn, Michigan, to produce impressive images of the age as a machine gone almost beserk:

> The little bucking trolley car loaded with metal bits and pieces strives to make headway through the workmen. Out of the light! They jump aside to let the hysterical little thing pass along. And hop! There it goes like a mad thing, clunking its way around belts and flywheels, taking the men their rations of fetters.[4]

John F. Carter saw the mood of the twenties as a legacy from the previous generation and stated this with yet another use of the driving metaphor:

[4] Louis-Ferdinand Céline, *Journey to the End of the Night* (London, 1950), p. 224.

They give us this Thing, knocked to pieces, leaky, red-hot,
threatening to blow up; and then they are surprised that we don't
accept it with the same attitude of pretty, decorous enthusiasm with
which they received it, 'way back in the eighteen nineties, nicely
painted, smoothly running, practically fool-proof. 'So simple that a
child can run it!' But the child couldn't steer it. He hit every possible
telegraph-pole, some of them twice, and ended with a head-on
collision for which *we* shall have to pay the fines and damages.[5]

Fitzgerald, whose first great success came with *This Side of Paradise* at the
very beginning of the decade, is often seen as both the spokesman and the
archetypal figure of the age and, writing in 1931, he characterized the
mood of the twenties as that of 'a whole race going hedonistic, deciding
on pleasure' and linked sexual emancipation with the growth of the
automobile industry.

The importance of the driving metaphor in *The Great Gatsby* is
discussed in some detail in the next section of this study but here the
general point should be made that the frequent mention of automobiles in
the novel gives an underpinning of mobility and speed to the cumulative
view of a world tottering on the edge of disintegration:

> His wife and mistress, until an hour ago secure and inviolate, were
> slipping precipitately from his control. Instinct made him step on the
> accelerator . . . (131).

Speed involves the passing of time, and Gatsby, like most Romantic
artists, must seek to destroy or at least readjust time in order to seize upon
the ideal. An example from Keats will suggest how time can distort and
betray the artist's vision. In 'Ode to a Nightingale' the poet tries to move
from the world of time ('Where youth grows pale, and spectre-thin, and
dies') to the timeless world of the nightingale's song, timeless because it
has always been the same no matter at what point in history it has been
heard. He seems, in stanzas 6 and 7, to be achieving this transference but
the final word of stanza 7 'forlorn', which means not only 'sorrowful' but
also 'long past', reintroduces the idea of the passing of time in the real
world and so 'tolls' him back to his 'sole self', the human being in the
mortal and hence dying world.

[5] John F. Carter, Jr, '"These Wild Young People", by One of Them', *Atlantic
Monthly* CXXVI (September, 1920), p. 302. Reprinted in Malcolm Cowley and
Robert Cowley (eds), *Fitzgerald and the Jazz Age* (New York, 1966), p. 48.

Gatsby's quest is to attain, via his love for Daisy, a realm beyond time. By idealizing the moment he hopes to transform it into something deathless:

> 'I wouldn't ask too much of her,' I ventured. 'You can't repeat the past.'
>
> 'Can't repeat the past?', he cried incredulously. 'Why of course you can!' (117)

Gatsby
Repeat
the
past.

His problem is, in some ways, a reverse of that seen in Keats's poem. Whereas Keats tried to ally his time-bound song with the timeless song of the bird, Gatsby tries to 'wed his unutterable visions' to the 'perishable breath' of Daisy's song (118). If Gatsby's arch-opponent is time then Fitzgerald takes great pains to insist that that opponent is always standing mockingly at Gatsby's side. There is an obvious irony in Gatsby's wish to repeat the past. Rather than defeating time by such a strategy he could only and endlessly repeat his own past, a largely sordid pastiche of Franklinesque philosophy, and America's past, a constant battle between dream and reality in which dream must always lose. References to the movement of 'real' time abound in the novel. Just before giving us the long list of frequent guests at Gatsby's parties, Nick notes:

> Once I wrote down on the empty spaces of a time-table the names of those who came to Gatsby's house that summer. It is an old time-table now, disintegrating at its folds, and headed 'This schedule in effect July 5th, 1922' (67).

The time-table is no longer 'in effect' nor is the 'ideal' time-table sought by Gatsby through the parties attended by all those 'grey names'. A stronger symbol of time-processes occurs when Gatsby and Daisy meet at Nick's house:

> Luckily the clock took this moment to tilt dangerously at the pressure of his head, whereupon he turned and caught it with trembling fingers, and set it back in place (93).

Gatsby apologizes to Nick who replies, 'It's an old clock'. Nick is amused because 'I think we all believed for a moment that it had smashed in pieces on the floor'. Their shared illusion presumably stems from the power of Gatsby's dream of Daisy made momentarily real by her presence, but although Gatsby almost succeeds in overturning time he doesn't quite make it. The clock is righted and time goes on. The juxtaposition of ideal and real time is beautifully described early in chapter 6:

The most grotesque and fantastic conceits haunted him in his bed at night. A universe of ineffable gaudiness spun itself out in his brain while the clock ticked on the washstand and the moon soaked with wet light his tangled clothes upon the floor (105).

The use of moonlight is brilliant in context, for moonlight makes things look magical but yet the moon rises and sets with relentless regularity; this is a powerful and perceptive synthesis of illusion and reality.

Time asserts its final superiority when Mr Gatz, appearing after his son's death, shows Nick the 'SCHEDULE' printed on the fly-leaf of an old copy of *Hopalong Cassidy*. While I have preferred throughout this study to treat *The Great Gatsby* as a novel with universal appeal it is at points such as this that the reader is reminded how firmly Fitzgerald wishes to align Gatsby's story with major American themes. The reference here is clearly to the 'bold and arduous project of arriving at moral perfection', outlined by Benjamin Franklin in his *Autobiography* (1791). As part of this project Franklin felt that each aspect of his business should have its allotted time and so wrote out a scheme of employment for the twenty-four hours of the day:

The Morning Question. What good shall I do this day?	5 6 7	Rise, wash and address Powerful Goodness! Contrive day's business, and take the resolution of the day; prosecute the present study, and breakfast.
	8 9 10 11	Work
Noon	12 1	Read, or overlook my accounts, and dine
	2 3 4 5	Work
Evening Question. What good have I done to-day?	6 7 8 9	Put things in their places. Supper, Music or diversion, or conversation. Examination of the day.

$$\text{Night} \quad \left.\begin{array}{c} 10 \\ 11 \\ 12 \\ 1 \\ 2 \\ 3 \\ 4 \end{array}\right\} \text{Sleep}$$

By linking Gatsby's scheme with Franklin's, Fitzgerald suggests what has happened, by the 1920s, to the great American 'rags-to-riches' dream—the notion, of which Franklin is usually seen as the archetype, that in the New World every individual is potentially a hero and that the normal Christian virtues can lead the poorest of youths to become a great (and wealthy) man. In the first part of the *Autobiography*, supposedly written to educate his son into the ways of the world, Franklin casts himself in the role of picaresque hero, altering the real facts of his life to suit this purpose. He becomes a poor boy with, as his only aids, his intelligence and the nature of the American experience in the early eighteenth century, when all possibilities appeared open to the right use of reason. Gatsby, too, is a poor boy with dreams, whose 'SCHEDULE' suggests an adherence to Franklin's Christian values but who, as his father says, 'rose up to his position in the East' (175), a corrupt world where progress can only be achieved through sordid underworld dealings:

> 'He and this Wolfsheim bought up a lot of side-street drug-stores here and in Chicago and sold grain alcohol over the counter. That's one of his little stunts. I picked him for a bootlegger the first time I saw him, and I wasn't far wrong.' (140)

Gatsby's rise can be measured by his successive friendships with Dan Cody and Meyer Wolfsheim. Cody is a Westerner with the same surname as Buffalo Bill, a self-made man gone soft who, as a 'pioneer debauchee . . . brought back to the Eastern seaboard the savage violence of the frontier brothel and saloon' (107). Cody, a genuine Western individualist who ends by pandering to the East's stereotyped view of the West, stands somewhere between the Dutch sailors viewing the 'fresh green breast of the new world' (187) and Wolfsheim. Wolfsheim is a Jew and hence to be associated with emigration from central Europe in the late nineteenth century. He comes to America with the rise of the cities and industrialization and fixes the 1919 World Series (something that

Gatsby's Rise (rags to riches)

really did happen). For Franklin, the rational Enlightenment man, time was something to which you could attune your efforts provided you spaced them properly; time was there to be used. Gatsby's schedule becomes pointless, since he needs to make his money quickly, both because he is desperate for Daisy and because the era demands such haste. He is used by time. Franklin's pragmatic dream turns to ashes in this novel as does Gatsby's Romantic dream. *The Great Gatsby* is often said to be about 'the American Dream' but perhaps there are two discernible dreams—the dream of material success and the dream of spiritual success.

Is Gatsby a complete failure in his attempt to arrest and transform time? One answer to this might emerge from an examination of the first of Gatsby's parties in chapter 3. How far, however, can Gatsby be seen as the creator of his party? People have become, by this time, so used to Gatsby's parties that each one takes on almost the air of a 'happening':

> I believe that on the first night I went to Gatsby's house I was one of the few guests who had actually been invited. People were not invited—they went there (47).

Gatsby has still not made a speaking appearance in the novel by the start of chapter 3 and at the end of the party he remains a lonely isolated figure:

> A sudden emptiness seemed to flow now from the windows and the great doors, endowing with complete isolation the figure of the host, who stood on the porch, his hand up in a formal gesture of farewell (62).

Looking back, not merely on the events but on his chronicle of events, Nick insists on their fleeting, temporary nature:

> I . . . wandered around rather ill at ease among swirls and eddies of people I didn't know . . . (47).

But he is the storyteller and the events are always related to us from his point of view, hence his reactions to the party must be our reactions and his reactions take the form, I would insist, of immersions in an imaginative experience which transcends the very material conditions which created it. There is an element of magic as well as medieval largesse in the food images:

> On buffet tables, garnished with glistening hors-d'œuvre, spiced baked hams crowded against salads of harlequin designs and pastry pigs and turkeys bewitched to a dark gold (45).

Fitzgerald here creates an effect greater than that of mere opulence. The transmutation of base reality has already begun; nothing is quite what it seems. The pigs are made of pastry, the turkeys are a colour rather from the world of aesthetics than the world of cuisine and the salads are of 'harlequin' designs, a word suggesting not merely a variety of colours but also masks and jokes. All in all this description serves as an admirable introduction to a remarkable paragraph which occurs shortly afterwards:

> The lights grow brighter as the earth lurches away from the sun, and now the orchestra is playing yellow cocktail music, and the opera of voices pitches a key higher. Laughter is easier minute by minute, spilled with prodigality, tipped out at a cheerful word. The groups change more swiftly, swell with new arrivals, dissolve and form in the same breath; already there are wanderers, confident girls who weave here and there among the stouter and more stable, become for a sharp, joyous moment the centre of a group, and then, excited with a triumph, glide on through the sea-change of faces and voices and colour under the constantly changing light (46).

The language here points to an apprehension of a world in constant movement, a creative flux where anything and everything is possible. One of Keats's favourite poetic devices is synaesthesia, whereby sensations are intermingled causing colours to be smelled or sounds to be tasted. In 'Ode to a Nightingale' the following lines occur:

> I cannot see what flowers are at my feet,
> Nor what soft incense hangs upon the boughs.

Flowers can certainly be seen, but incense is inhaled. Such a device is important to the Romantic writer since by it he suggests a total imaginative apprehension of experience and not merely a partial, sensual awareness. In *Gatsby* the device is used early ('yellow cocktail music') and later accentuated by 'the constantly changing light'. Nick is being subjected almost to psychedelic effects and the synaesthesia underlines the stimulus being received by his imagination. The effect of constant movement ('The groups change more swiftly, swell with new arrivals, dissolve and form in the same breath') on Nick's vision leads one to invoke Coleridge's view of the 'secondary imagination':

> It dissolves, diffuses, dissipates, in order to recreate; or where this process is rendered impossible, yet still, at all events, it struggles to idealize and unify.

That Nick, hitherto shown to us as a relatively prosaic young man, should be excited to such a vision at this point, suggests that he is embracing, osmotically, Gatsby's dream which encompasses and transmutes all sordid reality. This is further emphasized by the use of the Shakespearian term 'sea-change' in the final sentence. Gatsby's party has become like the sea in *The Tempest*, both an emblem and an agent of the power of Prospero, the magician/artist, to melt and recreate obdurate reality into a new and greater beauty. Of course, Nick, as the mediator, cannot become totally ensnared by this vision, otherwise he will become as trapped and fated as Gatsby, and so he underlines the retrospective nature of his description by his careful awareness (which Gatsby does not have) of the ruthless processes of time-bound reality. In order that Gatsby might create the right mood for his parties we are told, before the description of the gathering itself, that:

> . . . on Mondays eight servants, including an extra gardener, toiled all day with mops and scrubbing-brushes and hammers and garden-shears, repairing the ravages of the night before (45).

The specification of an exact number of servants with the neat inclusion of an 'extra' gardener (as though the normal contingent were inadequate to deal with the damage) and the extensive list of tools gives a mundane underpinning to the magical extravagance and suggests what human and material cost is involved. The single word 'ravages' operates in a more sinister manner, suggesting not merely wear and tear but almost bestial behaviour. The emphasis is similar to that when Keats points to the origin of the flowers at Lamia's wedding feast:

> Garlands of every green, and every scent
> From vales deflower'd, or forest-trees branch-rent.

'Ravages' in Fitzgerald's novel strongly emphasizes the unnatural aspects of such an entertainment, as does the introduction, quite appropriate for the 1920s, of automation:

> Every Friday five crates of oranges and lemons arrived from a fruiterer in New York—every Monday these same oranges and lemons left his back door in a pyramid of pulpless halves. There was a machine in the kitchen which could extract the juice of two hundred oranges in half an hour if a little button was pressed two hundred times by a butler's thumb (45).

Waste of food.

In the following paragraph the opulence of the cooked food is made to seem superb, while here the effect is both farcical and repellent and the reader is required to carry both propositions in his mind simultaneously. Fitzgerald once remarked that 'the test of a first-rate intelligence is the ability to hold two opposed ideas in the mind . . . and still retain the ability to function' (*Crack-Up* 39) and throughout the novel he insists, stylistically, that the reader look both ways at once, as when Daisy looks up at Nick 'with an absolute smirk on her lovely face' (24). Even in the 'yellow cocktail music' paragraph the word 'lurches' suggests something unbalanced, almost out of control, and the word occurs again later in the novel in connection with the metaphor of bad driving:

> . . . Gatsby's gorgeous car lurched up the rocky drive to my door and gave out a burst of melody from its three-noted horn (69).

Nevertheless the flux of Gatsby's party is basically creative rather than destructive (destruction being the gift of the Buchanans). A comparison with another American Romantic, Edgar Allan Poe, is instructive here. In one of his most successful stories, 'Ligeia', the 'mad' narrator is seeking to transcend the reality of his detested second wife, Rowena, and reunite himself with his dead first wife, Ligeia, whose description makes her ideal status quite clear:

> . . . the skin rivalling the purest ivory, the commanding extent and repose, the gentle prominence of the regions above the temple . . .

In order to accomplish this transformation he shuts himself up in one room of a remote Cornish abbey. The room conforms to what Poe would call 'arabesque reality'; nothing in it has relation to the outside world and everything seems to be in movement. The huge window has a single pane 'of a leaden hue'; the 'Saracenic' censor gives parti-coloured lights 'endued with a serpent vitality'; the tapestries and carpets are wrought with arabesque figures which change in appearance when the viewer moves and,

> The phantasmagoric effect was vastly heightened by the artificial introduction of a strong continual current of wind behind the draperies, giving a hideous and uneasy animation to the whole.

The flux so created enables the narrator, with the help of drugs, to obtain a visionary state whereby Ligeia, the ideal, returns to displace the real.[6]

[6] My reading of this Poe story has been influenced by an unpublished doctoral dissertation—David Ketterer, 'The Rationale of Deception in Poe' (University of Sussex, 1964).

Gatsby creates such an illusion at his party and it becomes reality and then makes normal reality seem curiously unreal. This may help to explain the odd incident where the drunken Owl-Eyes is discovered in Gatsby's library:

> 'What do you think?' he demanded impetuously.
> 'About what?'
> He waved his hand toward the book-shelves.
> 'About that. As a matter of fact you needn't bother to ascertain. I ascertained. They're real.' (51)

Gatsby's illusions are not mere sleight-of-hand but an attempt to build the ideal from reality:

> 'It's a bona-fide piece of printed matter. It fooled me. This fellow's a regular Belasco. It's a triumph. What thoroughness! What realism!' (52)

Treatment of Time.

One final example should make clear the complexity and brilliance of Fitzgerald's treatment of time. In chapter 5 Daisy pays her first visit to Gatsby's mansion and if the splendour of his wonder at her presence is signalled by the superb pile of shirts 'in many coloured disarray' (99) then the clandestine nature of their meeting is emphasized, in a manner reminiscent of T. S. Eliot, by Ewing Klipspringer's rendition of a tatty popular song, 'The Love Nest'. This ironic technique is repeated shortly afterwards:

> Outside the wind was loud and there was a faint flow of thunder along the Sound. All the lights were going on in West Egg now; the electric trains, men-carrying, were plunging home through the rain from New York. It was the hour of a profound human change, and excitement was generating on the air.
>
> > 'One thing's sure and nothing's surer
> > The rich get richer and the poor get—children.
> > In the meantime,
> > In between time—' (102).

The 'hour of a profound human change' modulates through the profound change occurring in the relationship between Gatsby and Daisy, through the more general and normal change associated with the hour of the day and with the exigencies of city life, to the cynical hedonism of the popular song. Perhaps three kinds of time are involved here: the ideal time of Gatsby and Daisy (though already subtly affected by real time), the real time of everyday activities and the 'between time' of the song.

The quality of Nick's vision of the first of Gatsby's parties may be emphasized by comparing it with his view of the party at Tom and Myrtle's apartment in chapter 2. Tom and Myrtle are sensualists whose awareness is rooted in the physical:

> 'He had on a dress suit and patent leather shoes, and I couldn't keep my eyes off him . . . When we came into the station he was next to me, and his white shirt-front pressed against my arm . . .' (42)

and therefore, although Nick gestures towards a mixture of attraction and repulsion in his reaction to the party,

> I was within and without, simultaneously enchanted and repelled by the inexhaustible variety of life. (42)

the occasion is time-bound,

> It was nine o'clock—almost immediately afterward I looked at my watch and found it was ten. (43)

and the flux is not creative but simply confusing,

> The little dog was sitting on the table looking with blind eyes through the smoke, and from time to time groaning faintly. People disappeared, reappeared, made plans to go somewhere, and then lost each other, searched for each other, found each other a few feet away (43).

That the emphasis in the chapter 2 party is on its decadence is made even more clear by the reading matter available in Tom and Myrtle's apartment:

> Several old copies of *Town Tattle* lay on the table together with a copy of *Simon Called Peter*, and some of the small scandal magazines of Broadway (35).

A seemingly incongruous juxtaposition proves less so when we remember that Fitzgerald felt that Robert Keable's best-seller, *Simon Called Peter* (1921) was an immoral book.

If time is a persistent enemy to Gatsby so too is its close relative, mortality, and once again, in analysing this, we must draw on the strong

Time → enemy to Gatsby.

Keatsian influence on this novel. One frequent signpost of mortality in Keats's poems, one indication of the destruction of the dream of beauty and the intrusion of or return to the mortal world of transience and death, is pallor, a human indication of suffering and loss. A major element of time is that it relentlessly invokes decay and the progress to the grave. The dreamer, cast out from the dream, might well echo Pope in speaking of 'this long disease, my life'. In 'La Belle Dame Sans Merci', the 'Knight at Arms' is found 'palely loitering' after his dream experience and we are told that he wakes to the 'cold hill side' (just as the process of time discovered the Grecian Urn to be a 'Cold Pastoral'). When Madeline in 'The Eve of St Agnes' is woken by Porphyro, she has difficulty adjusting her vision of the 'real' hero to that of the 'ideal' she has just been dreaming about and so his mortal nature is emphasized:

> How chang'd thou art! how pallid, chill, and drear!
> Give me that voice again, my Porphyro,
> Those looks immortal, those complainings dear!
> Oh leave me not in this eternal woe,
> For if thou diest, my love, I know not where to go.

Apollonius's steady gaze, the gaze of 'cold philosophy', begins to destroy the enchantress Lamia and so to destroy Lycius's dream of Lamia:

> Lycius then press'd her hand, with a devout touch,
> As pale it lay upon the rosy couch:
> 'Twas icy, and the cold ran through his veins.

Just as the clock ticks on throughout the novel, so mortality is always present and ready to intrude. Its presence is predominantly signalled by the imagery of the Valley of Ashes, a series of images whose principal feature is a ring of changes on the idea of pallor:

About half-way between West Egg and New York the motor road hastily joins the railroad and runs beside it for a quarter of a mile, so as to shrink away from a certain desolate area of land. This is a valley of *ashes*—a fantastic farm where *ashes* grow like wheat into ridges and hills and grotesque gardens; where *ashes* take the forms of houses and chimneys and rising *smoke* and, finally, with a transcendent effort, of *ash-grey* men, who move dimly and already crumbling through the *powdery* air. Occasionally a line of *grey* cars crawls along an invisible track, gives out a *ghastly* creak, and come to rest, and immediately the

The Valley of Ashes

ash-grey men swarm up with *leaden* spades and stir up an impenetrable *cloud*, which screens their obscure operations from your sight (29). [Italics mine.]

This description is bound to remind the reader of Eliot's *Waste Land* imagery ('I had not thought death had undone so many') and indeed the term 'waste land' is actually used by Fitzgerald:

The only building in sight was a small block of yellow brick sitting on the edge of the waste land . . . (30).

Like Eliot's Waste Land, the Valley of Ashes is a hideous image of a spiritually dead world, an objective correlative for the collapse of moral values after the war which underlines the boredom of Eliot's postwar generation and the hedonism and viciousness of Fitzgerald's. The Valley of Ashes lies half-way between West Egg and New York. Between the inherited acquisitiveness of the Buchanans and the 'self-made' acquisitiveness of Wolfsheim stand the victims of such a rapacious world. The Valley of Ashes lies close to the routes of American riches, the railroad track and the river, but is unable to partake of them. For those who feel that Fitzgerald, who became relatively rich in his mid-twenties, paid too much attention to the mentality of the rich, leisured class and not enough to the wider social problems of his day, the opening of chapter 2 might prove a sobering corrective. The Dutch sailors may have looked at the 'fresh, green breast of the new world' with a great capacity for wonder but, by the 1920s, the Valley of Ashes is a prominent result of American progress. The principal inhabitant of this land, Wilson, is described in terms which make him its most appropriate denizen:

. . . the proprietor himself appeared in the door of an office, wiping his hands on a piece of waste. He was a bland, spiritless man, anaemic, and faintly handsome (31).

Myrtle Wilson is seen as a reverse of a fairy's child and her reality as a woman is emphasized when we first meet her:

She was in the middle thirties, and faintly stout, but she carried her flesh sensuously as some women can (31).

But one effect of her sensuality is to accentuate her husband's pallor. Sensuality and pallor become, curiously, allied agents of an insurmountable reality. We have already seen that one of the primary

Ashes

functions of the Romantic imagination is persistently to transform the real world, continually change it into something new and dynamic, but the Waste Land remains as it is throughout the novel; it is incapable of transformation. When Nick first sees the awfulness of Wilson's garage he assumes that it is capable of transformation, that beauty will emerge from behind this dreary façade:

> It had occurred to me that this shadow of a garage must be a blind, and that sumptuous and romantic apartments were concealed overhead . . . (31).

The most prominent agent of such transformation is the eye of the beholder and so it is clearly significant that the eyes which overlook the waste land are sightless:

> The eyes of Doctor T. J. Eckleburg are blue and gigantic—their retinas are one yard high. They look out of no face, but, instead, from a pair of enormous yellow spectacles which pass over a non-existent nose. (29)

empty eyes presiding over an empty world. Wilson, after Myrtle's death, believes them to be the eyes of God which miss nothing:

> . . . 'and I said "God knows what you've been doing, everything you've been doing. You may fool me, but you can't fool God!"' Standing behind him, Michaelis saw with a shock that he was looking at the eyes of Doctor T. J. Eckleburg, which had just emerged, pale and enormous, from the dissolving night.
> 'God sees everything', repeated Wilson (166).

To Benjamin Franklin, as a Deist, the supremely useful aspect of his eighteenth-century God was that He was an 'absentee mechanic' who had created the world and allowed man full scope to perfect himself with a minimum of interference. No longer the Calvinist God whose hand could be seen in the most trivial of everyday occurrences, He now sat at some remove from His creation, watching benevolently as man struggled towards perfection. Fitzgerald's twentieth-century God, like the oculist, has simply gone; He is no longer watching.

To arrest time the Romantic artist must seek to transform reality into the ideal world of which the real is but a shadow. As we have seen, this is often accomplished by a merging of the senses which denies the categorization the rational mind gives to reality. Nick suggests that

'Jay Gatsby . . . sprang from his Platonic conception of himself' (105);
he attempts, that is, to live up to an ideal notion of himself which he has
divorced, dangerously, from the sordid reality in which he is embedded.
When Nick describes the last occasion on which he saw Gatsby alive he
speaks of Gatsby standing alone in his 'gorgeous pink rag of a suit' (160)
and emphasizes the astounding mixture of purity and sin that went to make
up Gatsby's character:

> The lawn and drive had been crowded with the faces of those who
> guessed at his corruption—and he had stood on those steps, concealing
> his incorruptible dream, as he waved them goodbye.

His Romantic dream separates him completely from the herd which
attends his parties but his sinister ways of obtaining money tie him firmly
to such people, force him to surround himself with them and so,
unconsciously, admit his kinship with them.

The 'Platonic' nature of Gatsby's vision is brilliantly demonstrated in
Nick's reconstruction of Gatsby's feelings at the time he is murdered.
Wilson's progress towards finding Gatsby takes on the inevitability of
fate; reality is closing in (very well suggested in Jack Clayton's 1974
film):

> The police, on the strength of what he said to Michaelis, that he 'had a
> way of finding out', supposed that he spent that time going from
> garage to garage thereabouts, inquiring for a yellow car. On the other
> hand, no garage man who had seen him ever came forward, and
> perhaps he had an easier, surer way of finding out what he wanted to
> know (167).

The last sentence here has a hint of the supernatural about Wilson's
progress. Now he takes on most conspicuously that symbolic role
prepared for in his first appearance. Nick has anticipated Gatsby:

> . . . and I tossed half-sick between grotesque reality and savage,
> frightening dreams. (153)

and then we join Gatsby's final moments:

> . . . he must have felt that he had lost the old warm world, paid a high
> price for living too long with a single dream. He must have looked up
> at an unfamiliar sky through frightening leaves and shivered as he
> found what a grotesque thing a rose is and how raw the sunlight was

upon the scarcely created grass. A new world, material without being real, where poor ghosts, breathing dreams like air, drifted fortuitously about . . . like that ashen, fantastic figure gliding toward him through the amorphous trees (168).

The sky is 'unfamiliar' because it is a real sky and the reality of the leaves (they are only leaves) is what makes them frightening. The reality of the Valley of Ashes has already been seen as 'grotesque' and after Gatsby's death the ignorance of the newspaper reports, ostensibly purveying facts, is similarly described. The nightmare of Gatsby's forced return to the real world consequent on the death of his dream is superbly encapsulated by the word 'raw', for this suggests pure, unadulterated reality which must possess a cutting edge when forced on the attention of the dreamer. The sunlight is 'raw' because it is the thing itself; naked reality incapable of transformation and thus totally inimical to the Romantic dream. It is, then, entirely appropriate that Wilson, a real man from a real world shooting live bullets from a real gun, should be described as though he were a phantom.

In Keats's 'Lamia' the real world which destroys the enchantment is seen as conspiratorial:

> As men talk in a dream, so Corinth all,
> Throughout her palaces imperial,
> And all her populous streets and temples lewd,
> Mutter'd, like tempest in the distance brew'd,
> To the wide-spreaded night above her towers.

and Appollonius, the voice of cold reason, assumes the aspect of a phantom:

> . . . but tonight he seems
> The ghost of folly haunting my sweet dreams.

After the death of Myrtle, Nick peers in through the window at Tom and Daisy reunited in their fear:

> They weren't happy, and neither of them had touched the chicken or the ale—and yet they weren't unhappy either. There was an unmistakable air of natural intimacy about the picture, and anybody would have said that they were conspiring together (152).

They 'conspire' to make Gatsby their scapegoat, so breaking his enchantment with Daisy which led to his quixotic gesture of taking the

). Gatsby – scapegoat.

Daisy — selfish. cruel. lazy.

blame for Myrtle's death. Since, as we have seen in the description of the first party at Gatsby's, the ideal involves flux and transformation, the real is frequently identified, for Nick, by hard, physical distinctiveness. Tom Buchanan's physique is early insisted on:

> Not even the effeminate swank of his riding clothes could hide the enormous power of that body—he seemed to fill those glistening boots until he strained the top lacing, and you could see a great pack of muscle shifting when his shoulder moved under his thin coat. It was a body capable of enormous leverage—a cruel body. (13)

as is Myrtle's; and the destruction of the dream by physical weight is brilliantly conveyed by the device of repeating an image but changing the context and perception of that image; for when Nick first sees Daisy and Jordan a sense of their almost enchanted beauty and freedom is created:

> The only completely stationary object in the room was an enormous couch on which two young women were buoyed up as though upon an anchored balloon. They were both in white, and their dresses were rippling and fluttering as if they had just been blown back in after a short flight around the house. (14)

but when he sees them again in a similar position he has begun to realize the appalling fragility of Gatsby's vision and can himself see more clearly Daisy's selfishness and Jordan's dishonesty:

> Daisy and Jordan lay upon an enormous couch, like silver idols weighing down their own white dresses against the singing breeze of the fans.
>
> 'We can't move', they said together (121).

PURE

In the first description the white dresses seem to be part of the purity of the ladies as Nick sees them, an inextricable element of their almost ethereal beauty. In the second description the dresses cover an essential hardness and materialism suggested both by 'silver' and by 'idols' (idles?). Ethereal creatures can fly like birds, earth-bound creatures are prevented from moving by their own grossness. They are too burdened by their own reality.

A larger use of this technique of differentiation by repetition occurs in the descriptions of the two parties given by Gatsby. In between the two Nick gives us, at the beginning of chapter 4, a long list of the people who regularly came out to savour Gatsby's hospitality. What is the point of such a long list? On one level it gives a clear indication of the social distinctions between the two Long Island communities. East Egg, where the Buchanans live, is the stronghold of inherited wealth and West Egg, where Gatsby lives, is the home of the *nouveaux riches*. Hence the West Egg list is much more of a 'melting pot' with Irish names (Mulready and Muldoon), Germanic and Eastern European (Schoen, Gulick), Mediterranean (Legros) and Jewish (Cohen and Schwartz). Besides this aspect, the cumulative effect of the lists is surely unpleasant. East Egg includes the 'Leeches' and Dr 'Civet' (a civet is a predatory feline creature) while West Egg has 'James B. ("Rot-Gut") Ferret' and the 'Catlips'. While New York offers the 'Smirkes', East Egg produces 'Mrs Ulysses Swett'. Milton R. Stern[7] remarks that this list contains debased famous names like 'Stonewall Jackson Abrams' and 'a man named Bunsen'. Fitzgerald's technique of yoking the sublime and the silly, as in 'the Willy Voltaires' and 'Mrs Ulysses Swett', creates an interesting link with Charles Dickens who, in *Martin Chuzzlewit* (1844), similarly comments on America's ludicrous sense of its own 'modern' greatness by creating the characters Jefferson Brick and Hannibal Chollop. Moreover, in *The Great Gatsby*, their ambience is unsavoury. Civet drowns, Clarence Endive fights, Snell goes to prison, Muldoon's brother strangles his wife and Henry L. Palmetto jumps in front of a subway train. It can, in addition, hardly be an accident that the first name on the East Egg list is 'Chester Becker' and ten pages later Wolfsheim is telling Nick about a gangster named Becker who was sent to the electric chair. The long list, then, substantially underlines the darker elements in that rich society which so fascinated its creator. The animality and suicidal impulses intermingled with the hedonism of the 1920s become quite clear. Fitzgerald is, no doubt, having a good deal of fun here as well as drawing on his extensive experience of Long Island society, but the crucial impact of this list is Keatsian—an intrusion of mean reality into the earlier possibilities of enchantment. In 'Lamia' Lycius himself helps to destroy Lamia's enchantment by insisting on inviting his Corinthian friends to a wedding feast. Keats refers to these brutal eruptions of reality as 'dreadful guests' and 'the gossip rout' and this helps us to understand what happens at the second party. Here Nick is with Tom as well as Daisy and their presence prevents him from entering the enchanted world:

[7] Milton R. Stern, *The Golden Moment* (Urbana, 1970), pp. 217–20.

There were the same people, or at least the same sort of people, the
same profusion of champagne, the same many-coloured, many-keyed
commotion, but I felt an unpleasantness in the air, a pervading
harshness that hadn't been there before . . . It is invariably saddening
to look through new eyes at things upon which you have expended
your own powers of adjustment (111).

Nick sees the party through Daisy's eyes and not through his own.
Daisy's eyes are incapable of participating in any Romantic
transformation since she retains too much of a hard core of selfish
snobbery. She is 'appalled by West Egg' (114):

. . . appalled by its raw vigour that chafed under the old euphemisms
and by the too obtrusive fate that herded its inhabitants along a short-
cut from nothing to nothing (114).

The reader may like to note here that the word 'raw', when transferred
from Gatsby's perceptions to Daisy's, becomes a somewhat less sinister
way of describing reality. Here the 'rawness' of West Egg indicates a
vitality lacking in East Egg; a vitality (akin to Myrtle's) which offends
Daisy and which Gatsby fatally ignores. Fitzgerald published a short
story called 'Absolution' in the American Mercury in June 1924, a story
which he had originally intended to use as part of the novel. Writing to
John Jamieson in 1934 he made this clear:

It might interest you to know that a story of mine, called 'Absolution'
in my book All the Sad Young Men was intended to be a picture of his
[Gatsby's] early life, but that I cut it because I preferred to preserve the
sense of mystery (528).

In this story a young, emotionally-disturbed priest, Father Schwartz,
offers the advice to a boy, Rudolph Miller, that he should go and watch a
fair at night, from a distance, 'like a big yellow lantern on a pole'; but he
warns him, 'don't get up close . . . because if you do you'll only feel the
heat and the sweat and the life.' (Bernice 91) This advice, of course,
mirrors the priest's own struggle between the ideal, the need for a
complete mystical union with God, and the real, the blonde, earthy
Nordic girls:

Legs were shaped under starchless ginghams, and rims of the necks of
dresses were warm and damp. For five hours now hot fertile life had
burned in the afternoon (Bernice 92).

In this story Fitzgerald pays a moving tribute to the intense difficulties of the priestly life as well as foreshadowing the similar difficulties to be encountered by Rudolph (Gatsby), the Minnesota small-town boy with a collection of Alger books and a father who worships James J. Hill.

As the wedding guests near Lamia's magically erected house Keats prompts our sympathies with the words 'The herd approach'd', suggesting their physicality and inability to apprehend the ideal. Fitzgerald uses the same noun here to suggest the same attributes but also to suggest, ironically, that Daisy cannot recognize her kinship with this 'herd'. She, Tom, and the leisured class they represent are all going 'along a short-cut from nothing to nothing'. At all events Daisy, when not viewed from Gatsby's perspective, is allied to her husband by her snobbery and hence sees everything as real and awful, forcing Nick to do the same, so that for him the evening turns 'septic' (113).

In the poetry of Keats and the stories of Poe the search for ideality often involves a woman of surpassing beauty who may also be dangerous. The relationship of these women to the world of the ideal is mirrored in their descriptions:

> I met a lady in the meads
> Full beautiful, a faery's child;
> Her hair was long, her foot was light,
> And her eyes were wild.

> A virgin purest lipp'd, yet in the lore
> Of love deep learned to the red heart's core.

In Keats's work these creatures do not represent the ideal in themselves but rather they offer an entrance, both alluring and frightening, to the ideal world. Gatsby is first seen stretching out his arms towards the green light in the distance. This, to be sure, may be the light at the end of the Buchanans' dock but as the novel progresses it becomes a symbol of the hopeless yearning for a total beauty which men can never fully achieve, what Shelley called 'the desire of the moth for the star'. Daisy's maiden name is 'Fay', a word meaning 'fairy' (as in 'Morgan le Fay'), and to Gatsby she is the fairy's child in a Keatsian romance he has created for himself:

'Her voice is full of money', he said suddenly. That was it. I'd never understood before. It was full of money—that was the inexhaustible

charm that rose and fell in it, the jingle of it, the cymbal's song of it . . .
High in a white palace the king's daughter, the golden girl . . . (126).

Even here Gatsby is unable to apprehend Daisy as totally removed from
the mercenary world. Instead he makes the heroic but impossible effort to
merge the time-bound (material) and the timeless (spiritual), in the
manner of 'Ode to Autumn'. This persistent attempt both enhances his
heroic status and dooms him irrevocably. Like Poe's heroines, Daisy is
related to the hero's past, to something he believes he once had and which
reality took away from him, to those 'fantastic' reveries of his youth:

> For a while these reveries provided an outlet for his imagination; they
> were a satisfactory hint of the unreality of reality, a promise that the
> rock of the world was founded securely on a fairy's wing (106).

This aspect of *The Great Gatsby* had already been worked over by
Fitzgerald in two stories he had published before the novel—'Winter
Dreams', published in *Metropolitan Magazine* in December 1922 and 'The
Sensible Thing', published in *Liberty* in July 1924. In addition to his
obvious interest in Romantic writing, Fitzgerald was much affected by
the grimly realistic Naturalist writers in America and sometimes felt that
there was insufficient realism in his work. In these two stories the
Romantic dream is firmly if sadly defeated. In 'Winter Dreams' Dexter
Green is a caddy who loves the belle of the local golf club, Judy Jones. He
becomes rich for her and she rejects him and is subsequently ill-treated by
her husband. At the end Dexter reflects:

> The gates were closed, the sun was gone down, and there was no
> beauty but the grey beauty of steel that withstands all time. Even the
> grief he could have borne was left behind in the country of illusion, of
> youth, of the richness of life, where his winter dreams had flourished
> (*Bernice* 59).

In 'The Sensible Thing' George O'Kelly gives up his advertising job in
New York and goes South to try to woo and win Jonquil Cary. Tearfully
she throws him over and he goes to South America and becomes rich.
Several months later he comes back to see her and, firstly, discovers a
change in her house:

> . . . there was no cloud of magic hovering over its roof and issuing
> from the windows of the upper floor (*Bernice* 71).

Gatsby tries desperately to turn the present back to the past.

George gets his girl in the end but realizes that something has been lost since his immersion in the materialist world:

> . . . a trust, a warmth had gone forever. The sensible thing—they had done the sensible thing. He had traded his youth for strength and carved success out of despair. But with his youth, life had carried away the freshness of his love (*Bernice* 73).

Both Dexter Green and George O'Kelly come to accept, sadly but definitely, that the dream is in the past and that the capacity for wonder has vanished through the process of time and the involvement in an acquisitive, time-bound society. The same awareness ought to have been Gatsby's but, remarkably, he refuses to take the 'sensible' view and, NS instead, clings defiantly to the power of his imagination to turn the present back into the past. As a Romantic he tries to escape the naturalistic implications of the manner in which society has moulded him and determined his position.

For Poe, a writer who eschews social comment, it is possible to recapture this past ideal, as in 'Ligeia' and 'The Oval Portrait', but only at the cost of destroying the human present. This destruction is not viewed from a moral perspective. For Gatsby the very presence of Daisy, her tangible relation to a tangible world, effectively prevents an entry into the ideal world. Daisy is suddenly made real for him when one of her social roles, that of mother, is forced on his attention by the presence of her child:

> Afterward he kept looking at the child with surprise. I don't think he had ever really believed in its existence before (123).

Still, Daisy's close relationship to Gatsby's concept of the ideal is signified, as with the enchantresses in Keats's poems, by the great power which resides in her voice and song. It is Lamia's song which seduces Lycius:

> And as he from one trance was wakening
> Into another, she began to sing,
> Happy in beauty, life, and love, and every thing,
> A song of love, too sweet for earthly lyres,
> While, like held breath, the stars drew in their
>   panting fires.

For Keats, as Earl Wasserman[8] points out, song represents one of the stages on the way out of mortality into the ideal world. The effect of Daisy's voice is early remarked upon by Nick:

> . . . there was an excitement in her voice that men who had cared for her found difficult to forget: a singing compulsion, a whispered 'Listen', a promise that she had done gay, exciting things just a while since and that there were gay, exciting things hovering in the next hour (15–16).

This later becomes a 'deathless song' and then she does sing:

> Daisy began to sing with the music in a husky, rhythmic whisper, bringing out a meaning in each word that it had never had before and would never have again (115).

For Nick her song is redolent of 'her warm human magic' (115), but it is perhaps insufficiently ethereal for Gatsby; its very humanness betrays his dream.

Romantic adoration of women is age-old and receives one of its profoundest expressions in the literature of courtly love. Courtly love, influenced as it was by aspects of worship of the Virgin Mary, insisted on the fact that worship of the lady led to ennoblement of the lover's character. In Arthurian legends the knight could undertake the trials of chivalry in greater heart because of his love for the lady. Yet there was a paradox at the heart of this doctrine since the relationship had to be extra-marital and hence the movement came to seem to condone adultery and was thus branded as blasphemous. Courtly love, indeed, was seen to involve an ideal relationship only in so far as that relationship was extra-marital. Marriage was a contract entered into for the sake of social comfort and economic security and therefore must always be 'real', never 'ideal'. There can be no magic about the riches poured upon Daisy by her husband, only a straightforward statement of their material value:

> He came down with a hundred people in four private cars, and hired a whole floor of the Muhlback Hotel, and the day before the wedding he gave her a string of pearls valued at three hundred and fifty thousand dollars (82).

Often the knights in Arthurian romance are seeking for something beyond the love of a beautiful woman. Their quest is for the Holy Grail,

[8] Earl R. Wasserman, *The Finer Tone: Keats' Major Poems* (Baltimore, 1967).

the cup used by Christ at the Last Supper, the cup in which Joseph of Arimathea caught some of Christ's blood at the Crucifixion and which came to stand for that perfection by which the seeker becomes joined to God's love and grace. The knight whose worship of the woman has led him into illicit passion, like Lancelot, becomes unworthy to see the Grail and so is blinded by its light. Only a pure knight, such as Galahad, can attain the correct vision.

Following this pattern (and perhaps influenced by T. S. Eliot's use of the Grail Quest in *The Waste Land*) Fitzgerald has Nick liken Gatsby's pursuit of Daisy to the Grail Quest:

> He had intended, probably, to take what he could and go—but now he found he had committed himself to the following of a grail. (155)

and the connections are very important. It becomes increasingly clear that Gatsby's dream is larger than Daisy herself and this point receives its finest, most evocative statement at the end of chapter 5:

> There must have been moments even that afternoon when Daisy tumbled short of his dreams—not through her own fault, but because of the colossal vitality of his illusion. It had gone beyond her, beyond everything. He had thrown himself into it with a creative passion, adding to it all the time, decking it out with every bright feather that drifted his way (102–3).

Gatsby's dream.

His dream, as we have seen, is betrayed by its inability to transcend or escape the physical world which is redolent of passion and betrayal. We are led to imagine, in simple terms, that Gatsby has worshipped Daisy from afar for some five years. Yet we discover, late in the novel, that their relationship did have a physical basis:

> So he made the most of his time. He took what he could get, ravenously and unscrupulously—eventually he took Daisy one still October night, took her because he had no real right to touch her hand (155).

The language of this passage is most significant. The first sentence seeks to establish Gatsby as a seedy twentieth-century version of Benjamin Franklin. At this point there is no question of transcending the time-bound world. As one of its denizens Gatsby uses its minutes to further his plans and these plans involve the material world's attributes of aggression and manipulation. The words 'ravenously' and 'unscrupulously' are, to

Gatsby - concept of Time
Time is sex ~ Used to further his plans
→ Material world.

say the least, unambiguous. Gatsby does not merely 'make love' to Daisy, he 'takes' her, so treating her as an object and behaving very like Tom Buchanan who walks in an 'alert, aggressive way' (185) and smashes up 'things and creatures' (186). Thus the Gatsby/Daisy relationship is seen to be much more paradoxical than at first appeared and to contain within itself, from almost its earliest days, the seeds of its own destruction. Gatsby's knightly gesture of protecting Daisy occurs after he has been in a car with someone else's wife (as Tom Buchanan had been at the time of his accident) and his dream can only continue by a desperate and selfish disregard for the human beings involved. One can trace a pattern of this dismissal of the human aspect throughout Gatsby's behaviour. This pattern can be seen in the emphasis on his possessions during the tour of his house, through the over-closeness of Daisy's presence:

> It had seemed as close as a star to the moon. Now it was again a green light on a dock. His count of enchanted objects had diminished by one. (100)

through his atonishment at the very existence of Daisy's child, through the awful ambivalence of the remark that 'Her voice is full of money' (126), through Gatsby's incomprehension at Daisy's ability to love more than one person:

> She began to sob helplessly. 'I did love him once—
> but I loved you too.'
> Gatsby's eyes opened and closed.
> 'You loved me *too*?' he repeated. (139)

and culminates in an extraordinary remark by Gatsby:

> 'Of course she might have loved him just for a minute, when they were first married—and loved me more even then, do you see?'
> Suddenly he came out with a curious remark.
> 'In any case', he said, 'it was just personal.'
> What could you make of that, except to suspect some intensity in his conception of the affair that couldn't be measured? (158)

The remark may appear curious but it is quite in keeping with Gatsby's illusion. His view of Daisy's love for Tom as 'personal' is the Romantic's defence mechanism. By so designating her feelings he can see that love as an aberration caused by immersion in the time-bound, corrupt world. Such a love is merely physical and of the moment; it cannot match the ideal love which he has woven around Daisy in his dreams. I believe Dan H. McCall[9] is making a similar point when he remarks that in this novel, as in the poetry of Keats, the greatest threat to the dream of total beauty is an overabundance of beauty. When Lycius invites the Corinthians to his wedding feast Lamia provides great abundance for them:

> Garlands of every green, and every scent
> From vales deflower'd, or forest-trees branch-rent,
> In baskets of bright osier'd gold were brought
> High as the handles heap'd, to suit the thought
> Of every guest; that each, as he did please,
> Might fancy-fit his brows, silk-pillow'd at his ease.

Quite apart from the rapacity suggested in the opening lines of this passage there is an overall sense of an opulence which cloys and satiates; a beauty which leaves too little to the imagination and so must effectively prevent the recreation of the ideal. Lycius cannot maintain his dream under such conditions for the Romantic hero has enormous difficulty in maintaining the coherence of his vision if he stands in too close proximity to the materials of that vision. While beauty (and Daisy) are symbolized for Gatsby by the green light in the distance there is a security in the vision. When at last he has Daisy the awful processes of mortality have set in. Even before he meets Daisy at Nick's house his doom is clearly prefigured in his appearance. Nick finds him on the doorstep, 'pale as death' (92).

[9] Dan H. McCall, '"The Self-Same Song That Found a Path": Keats and *The Great Gatsby*', *American Literature* XLII (1970–71), p. 523.

3 Nick

The narrative scheme of *The Great Gatsby* has much in common with those of two other major works of fiction, Herman Melville's *Moby-Dick* (1851) and Joseph Conrad's *Heart of Darkness*. Each novel begins with a young narrator who seems particularly suited, because of a mood of boredom and indecisiveness, to embark on a journey which will teach him fundamental truths about the human condition. Ishmael begins by insisting on the need to go to sea to rid oneself of 'humors':

> . . . whenever it is a damp, drizzly November in my soul . . . then, I account it high time to get to sea as soon as I can (93).

Marlow needs a voyage to shake off boredom:

> . . . I was loafing about, hindering you fellows in your work and invading your houses, just as though I had got a heavenly mission to civilize you. It was very fine for a time, but after a bit I did get tired of resting (11).

Similarly, Nick Carraway returns to the Mid-West after participating in the Great War and is confined by its morality and made fretful:

> Instead of being the warm centre of the world, the Middle West now seemed like the ragged edge of the universe (9).

In each case this learning process becomes associated with the movement of the narrator towards a mysterious, charismatic figure who towers above the other characters around him, not simply through force of personality but also through being surrounded by an aura of mystery emanating from his essential *separateness*. Each author creates suspense by delaying the entry of this charismatic figure. Ahab does not enter into sight in *Moby-Dick* until chapter 28, which is called, appropriately enough, 'Ahab'. This occurs some twenty-two per cent of the way through the novel. The equivalent figures for *Heart of Darkness* and *The Great Gatsby* would be, respectively, seventy-five per cent and twenty-five per cent (not counting Gatsby's first, silent appearance at the end of chapter 1). This suspense is emphasized by having the narrator, before his initial meeting with the mysterious figure, regaled with wild rumours concerning that figure. Ishmael is pestered by the weird prophet, Elijah:

> But nothing about that thing that happened to him off Cape Horn, long ago, when he lay like dead for three days and nights; nothing about that deadly skrimmage with the Spaniard afore the altar in Santa? —heard nothing about that, eh? (189)

Marlow, as he is lying on the deck of his steamboat one evening, has his imagination titillated by hearing scraps of a conversation between the nephew and the uncle concerning Kurtz:

> 'Military   post—doctor—two   hundred   miles—quite   alone now—unavoidable   delays—nine   months—no   news—strange rumours' (46).

Similarly Nick meets, first, a woman at Myrtle's apartment who believes Gatsby to be a 'nephew or cousin of Kaiser Wilhelm's' (38) and, second, a girl at Gatsby's first party who has been told that 'he killed a man once' (50).

   This technique may usefully be termed *Gothic*, for the Gothic novel, forming as it does part of the Romantic movement of the late eighteenth and early nineteenth centuries, often depended for its success on the creation of a central character who, through his abundant energy and will-power, emphasized both the positive and negative aspects of Romanticism's attention to the potentialities of the individual ego. It may seem initially preposterous to consider Gatsby alongside such 'Byronic' heroes as Schedoni, Manfred or Heathcliff since Gatsby appears to be so amiable, so anxious to be liked and to have the appearance of 'an elegant young roughneck' rather than the spectre-thin dark man with the piercing eyes well known to all lovers of the Gothic novel. He is not, like the Byronic hero, tortured by an overwhelming sense of sin and guilt, but like the central figures of the Gothic novel he is driven by a gigantic compulsion emanating from the past; like them he has a total (and doomed) commitment to the one he loves; like them he possesses a code of life which is clear-cut yet profound; and, like them, he is monumentally self-reliant. The positive aspects of Romantic individualism may be seen in Shelley's appraisal of Milton's Satan:

> Milton's Devil as a moral being is as far superior to his God, as one who perseveres in some purpose which he has conceived to be excellent in spite of adversity and torture is to one who in the cold security of undoubted triumph inflicts the most horrible revenge upon his enemy . . .

and the negative aspects in a statement by Coleridge:

> But in its utmost abstraction and consequent state of reprobation, the will becomes Satanic pride and rebellious self-idolatry in the relations of the spirit to itself, and remorseless despotism relatively to others . . .

Both Shelley and Coleridge are talking about the same attributes of a Romantic hero, so it is hardly surprising that the foremost attitude to that hero in Gothic fiction (usually the heroine's) is ambiguous and confused and can best be described as 'attraction/repulsion'. This term aptly describes the attitudes of Ishmael, Marlow and Nick to the charismatic figures in these three works. Each is attracted to that figure's power and courage, especially since these attributes are persistently contrasted to the materialism and shallowness of many of the surrounding characters. Here is Nick at the opening of the novel:

> Only Gatsby, the man who gives his name to this book, was exempt from my reaction—Gatsby, who represented everything for which I have an unaffected scorn. If personality is an unbroken series of successful gestures, then there was something gorgeous about him, some heightened sensitivity to the promises of life, as if he were related to one of those intricate machines that register earthquakes ten thousand miles away . . . No—Gatsby turned out all right at the end; it is what preyed on Gatsby, what foul dust floated in the wake of his dreams that temporarily closed out my interest in the abortive sorrows and short-winded elations of men (8).

So, with more of horror than elation, does Marlow react to Kurtz's vision:

> This is the reason why I affirm that Kurtz was a remarkable man. He had something to say. He said it. Since I had peeped over the edge myself, I understand better the meaning of his stare, that could not see the flame of the candle, but was wide enough to embrace the whole universe, piercing enough to penetrate all the hearts that beat in the darkness (101).

The hero is also attracted to that single-mindedness which helps to illuminate the mortal condition:

> Gatsby believed in the green light, the orgiastic future that year by year recedes before us. It eluded us then, but that's no matter—tomorrow we will run faster, stretch out our arms further . . . And one fine morning— (188)

just as Ishmael's attraction to Ahab is prefigured in the first sight he catches of that awful figure:

> There was an infinity of firmest fortitude, a determinate, unsurrenderable wilfulness, in the fixed and fearless, forward dedication of that glance (220).

Repulsion arises from a contemplation of these same attributes from a different viewpoint—a sense of the total isolation of the Romantic figure and the resultant warping of the ego present in Ahab's sultanism, Kurtz's madness and Gatsby's corruption. In each novel the narrator has to witness the human cost of such single-mindedness. Ahab's determination to kill the White Whale results in the loss of the *Pequod* and all her crew except Ishmael. In Kurtz's case nothing so catastrophic actually happens but, given the classic addendum to his report ('Exterminate all the brutes!'), we are left in little doubt that, had he lived, it could have done. In *The Great Gatsby* human cost is also involved and that human cost is related to Gatsby's inextricable connection with the vicious underpinning of capitalist society. One might argue that Melville had an ambivalent view of whaling. *Moby-Dick* is, on one level, a paean to American enterprise. Melville selects an industry in which Americans were already paramount by the mid-nineteenth century, but the essential heroism of the enterprise also emphasizes the cruelty of American pioneering. James Fenimore Cooper's *The Pioneers* (1823) had already indicated the appalling waste involved in the relentless movement of civilization ever westward and Melville suggests in his novel that the whaling venture is a mixture of honest industry and wild greed. Ahab's megalomania itself is a true microcosm of this mixture of motives within the larger society, though his greed is for vengeance rather than material gain. Kurtz is made to seem much greater than the muddle by which Conrad characterizes Belgian imperialism in the Congo but his very madness is an extension of that imperialist ethic. In *Heart of Darkness* the

Grove of Death becomes, like Fitzgerald's Valley of Ashes, an emblem of the greed and moral decay present in the materialist world:

> I avoided a vast artificial hole somebody had been digging on the slope, the purpose of which I found impossible to divine . . . I discovered that a lot of imported drainage-pipes for the settlement had been tumbled in there . . . It was a wanton smash-up . . . My purpose was to stroll into the shade for a moment; but no sooner within than it seemed to me I had stepped into the gloomy circle of some Inferno (23–4).

In both passages the predominant mood is one of death, decay and awful purposelessness. Robert Emmet Long,[1] noting this similarity, suggests that one purpose of both writers is to juxtapose the isolated hero against the ethics of a particular society, ethics which he transcends. This is true in part, but it should also be noted that both isolated heroes also belong, inescapably, to the ethics which they transcend. Kurtz is a part of Belgian imperialism and although Gatsby is much larger and greater than people like Buchanan and Wolfsheim the basis of his Romantic freedom is firmly located in their world; he is a crook. As with Isabel Archer in Henry James's *Portrait of a Lady* (1881), the economic basis of freedom becomes the direct means of his imprisonment. Isabel is free to choose because she has a fortune of seventy thousand pounds and she chooses to marry Gilbert Osmond who is attracted to her because she has this fortune. Gatsby makes a great deal of money by illegal methods in order to be free to claim Daisy and then dies because, in part, he is associated with a materialism which constantly attracts her.

The main agent of destruction is the automobile. Cars, as R. A. Corrigan has pointed out,[2] are always appropriate to their owners in this novel. Daisy, before she marries, dresses in white and drives 'a little white roadster' (81) to emphasize her purity, while Nick, the observer and moralist, drives 'an old Dodge' (9). Gatsby, of course, owns an enormous car. We have already seen that Gatsby is a peculiar mixture of heroic idealism and meretricious vulgarity and the description of his car points firmly to his rooted place in the materialist society:

[1] Robert Emmet Long, '*The Great Gatsby* and the Tradition of Joseph Conrad: Part II', *Texas Studies in Literature and Language* VIII, no. 3 (Fall, 1966), pp. 407–8.

[2] R. A. Corrigan, 'Somewhere West of Laramie, on the Road to West Egg: Automobiles, Fillies, and the West in *The Great Gatsby*', *Journal of Popular Culture* VII, no. 1 (Summer, 1973), pp. 156–7.

It was a rich cream colour, bright with nickel, swollen here and there
in its monstrous length with triumphant hat-boxes and supper-boxes
and tool boxes, and terraced with a labyrinth of wind-shields that
mirrored a dozen suns (70).

Nick, at the end, says of Daisy and Tom that 'they were very careless
people' (186), but this could just as easily be said of Gatsby. His dream is
based in underworld dealings which undermine American society and he
disrupts Daisy's life and must be held partly responsible when she runs
down Myrtle. Myrtle's personality is coarse and imitative but it is vital:

> Her face, above a spotted dress of dark blue crêpe-de-chine, contained
> no facet or gleam of beauty, but there was an immediately perceptible
> vitality about her as if the nerves of her body were continually
> smouldering (31).

It is hardly surprising that she walks 'through her husband as if he were a
ghost' (31). In her death she takes on a representative stature as life snuffed
out by the power and glitter of the rich society. When the car hits her it
rips loose her breast, the symbol of both sexuality and maternity. In her
death she gives up 'the tremendous vitality she had stored so long' and her
'thick dark blood' (144) mingles with the dust. Here she is contrasted to
her 'anaemic' husband who, as Dickens says of Bitzer, 'looked as though,
if he were cut, he would bleed white'.

   Images of cars and driving abound to the extent of taking on the
function of a continuous metaphor which emphasizes the moral basis of
the novel and relates this basis strongly to those of the two other novels
I have been discussing. One of the key chapters in *Moby-Dick* is
undoubtedly chapter 96. 'The Try-Works', where Ishmael's description
of the furnace for boiling down the whale's blubber is filled with infernal
imagery (the smoke is 'an argument for the pit', the pagan harpooners
stand like 'Tartarean shapes' and speak of 'unholy adventures' (533)) and
where Ishmael falls asleep at the helm, wakes up facing into the try-works
with the feeling that the ship is 'rushing from all havens astern' (534)
and only turns to prevent the ship from capsizing at the last moment. The
concluding three paragraphs of that chapter, as R. W. B. Lewis has
excellently argued, [3] read like a synopsis of the Blakeian journey from
innocence through experience to 'Higher Innocence'. This is, to some
extent, Ishmael's journey through the novel; and one reason, perhaps,

---

[3] R. W. B. Lewis, *The American Adam* (Chicago, 1959), pp. 131–42.

why he is the sole survivor is that he is able, in a crisis, to steer. Ahab, the captain, the ultimate steerer of the ship, dashes to pieces the quadrant, an instrument vitally necessary for navigation.

In *Heart of Darkness*, Marlow increasingly feels the lure of the primitive darkness surrounding his boat as he sails up the Congo, further and further from civilized existence. At one point he sees a crowd of naked natives dancing on the shore and admits his undeniable kinship with such atavism. Yet he does not join them because of his need to control the boat:

> I had no time. I had to mess about with white-lead and strips of woollen blanket helping to put bandages on those leaky steam-pipes—I tell you. I had to watch the steering, and circumvent those snags, and get the tin-pot along by hook or by crook. There was surface-truth enough in these things to save a wiser man (52).

Marlow cannot follow Kurtz into the abyss because of his adherence to 'surface-truth', that by which most people survive. Kurtz, on the other hand, 'had no restraint', like 'a tree swayed by the wind'.

Various examples of bad driving occur in *The Great Gatsby*. At the close of Gatsby's first party Nick finds that Owl Eyes has run his new coupé into a ditch after knocking off one of the wheels:

> 'But how did it happen? Did you run into the wall?'
> 'Don't ask me', said Owl Eyes, washing his hands of the whole matter. 'I know very little about driving—next to nothing. It happened, and that's all I know.' (60–61)

Shortly after that Nick admonishes Jordan Baker:

> 'You're a rotten driver', I protested. 'Either you ought to be more careful, or you oughtn't to drive at all.' (65)

and a stronger example of the link between bad driving and moral laxity occurs during one of Tom Buchanan's early forays into infidelity:

> A week after I left Santa Barbara Tom ran into a wagon on the Ventura road one night, and ripped a front wheel off his car. The girl who was with him got into the papers, too, because her arm was broken—she was one of the chambermaids in the Santa Barbara Hotel (83–4).

In both the literal and moral senses Tom's steering is incompetent just as Gatsby's moral inadequacies help towards Daisy's failure to steer the 'death car' properly:

'Well, first Daisy turned away from the woman toward the other car, and then she lost her nerve and turned back. The second my hand reached the wheel I felt the shock . . .' (150–51)

The principal steerer in the novel is, of course, Nick Carraway. He is introduced to us, at the start of the novel, as a careful man, the reverse of impulsive in his gestures and judgments ('I'm inclined to reserve all judgments' (7). Like Pip in Dickens's *Great Expectations* (1860–61), Nick tells his story some time after it has happened, with hindsight, so that its end is implicit in its beginning. Because he is such a man he will scorn the carelessness of Tom, but while he may prefer the carelessness of Gatsby he cannot imitate Gatsby's life-style, nor would he wish to. He is essentially a middle-man, seen between two exaggeratedly opposed value systems (opposed but not totally dissimilar) and he tries to steer a path somewhere between them. He is, therefore, like Ishmael and Marlow, a better steerer than most of the other characters in his story. Just after his remark to Jordan he says of himself:

. . . I am slow-talking and full of interior rules that act as brakes on my desires. (65)

and this is echoed in his final rejection of Jordan. As I mentioned in the introduction, some critics have seen this rejection as a sign of Nick's essential priggishness but it is an inevitable result of such a learning process as the novel unfolds for us. Nick's relationship with Jordan runs parallel with that of Gatsby and Daisy (on each of the two occasions when Nick sees Daisy on the couch Jordan is there alongside her, a sort of carbon-copy) but Nick has, by the end, an acute sense of Jordan's dishonesty. Her lies may seem trivial to us but, to Nick, they come to represent the fatal dishonesty implicit in a whole way of life, a way of life where a yawning gap has opened between appearance and reality:

. . . I suppose she had begun dealing in subterfuges when she was very young in order to keep that cool, insolent smile turned to the world and yet satisfy the demands of her hard jaunty body (64–5).[4]

---

[4] Jordan, like Tom, is seen to be physically *hard*. Both are athletes: Jordan is a well-known golfer and Gatsby, at his party, introduces Tom as 'Mr. Buchanan the polo player' (112). It could be argued that the dream of being a sporting hero (much more prevalent in the United States than in Europe) is a variant on the rags-to-riches theme. For treatments of this theme see Arthur Miller, *Death of a Salesman* (1949) and Bernard Malamud, *The Natural* (1952).

As several critics have pointed out, the name 'Jordan Baker' is an amalgamation of two popular makes of automobile in the 1920s. She is a 'bad driver' who can never be anything else:

> 'You said a bad driver was only safe until she met another bad driver? Well, I met another bad driver, didn't I? I mean it was careless of me to make such a wrong guess. I thought you were rather an honest, straightforward person. I thought it was your secret pride.'
>
> 'I'm thirty', I said. 'I'm five years too old to lie to myself and call it honour.' (184–5)

Nick has seen that Gatsby, in order to maintain his dream, has had persistently to lie to himself and call it honour and this has led to his last quixotic gesture of taking the blame for Myrtle's death:

> 'Well, I tried to swing the wheel——' He broke off, and suddenly I guessed at the truth.
>
> 'Was Daisy driving?'
>
> 'Yes', he said after a moment, 'but of course I'll say I was.' (100)

The trouble with such Romantic chivalry is that it creates idols out of fallible human beings; it is a basic distortion of truth and Nick has seen too much to accept it as a viable approach to life. In this connection it should be noted that Nick, very early in the novel, refers to a 'rather hard-boiled painting' (9) of his great-uncle that hangs in his father's office. His dismissal of Jordan can, I would suggest, be usefully linked to the distrust of women which is a recurrent feature of 'hard-boiled' American fiction in the late twenties and the thirties. A particularly interesting comparison can be made with Sam Spade's repudiation of Brigid O'Shaughnessy at the end of Dashiell Hammett's *The Maltese Falcon* (1930). The world of this novel is much bleaker than that of *The Great Gatsby* and is much closer to Hemingway's existentialist world. All idealist gestures are eschewed and Spade is seen as a laconic opportunist tying himself to a frayed code of duty more in order to find and hold a small personal area of light amid a welter of corruption, deceit and greed (symbolized by the figure of the bird) than from a belief in any order higher than the individual. Brigid represents a profound threat to the equilibrium of Spade's world since he finds himself falling in love with her even though she lies about everything (including her name) and uses romantic language which is totally divorced from meaning. His reiterated phrase in the concluding pages of the novel, 'I won't play the sap for you', [5] seems like an echo of Nick's final words to Jordan. Like Nick, Spade dare not surrender his hard-won equilibrium for a relationship in which Romantic diction and posturings are made to cover a fundamental dishonesty and lack of trust.

Despite this learning process it would be unsafe, however, to minimize the difficulties involved in interpreting the end of the novel. What point has Nick reached when he remarks,

> So we beat on, boats against the current, borne back ceaselessly into the past. (188)?

What is his state of mind during these final ponderings? In *Moby-Dick*, Ishmael is saved by clinging to a coffin made by Queequeg, the heathen with whom Ishmael has achieved a bond which cuts across race, culture and creed. Ishmael rejects the sultanism of Ahab and the facile piety of Starbuck in favour of human relationships within which you learn about yourself and others. His journey of discovery leads him to apprehend more fully than is allowed to most people that combination of terror and glory which constitutes the fullest sense of the word 'human'. An index of this learning process occurs in chapter 94 when Ishmael and his crew-mates are squeezing the sperm:

> Such an abounding, affectionate, friendly, loving feeling did this avocation beget; that at last I was continually squeezing their hands, and looking up into their eyes sentimentally; as much as to say,— Oh! my dear fellow beings, why should we longer cherish any social acerbities, or know the slightest ill-humour or envy! (527)

This is also true of Marlow. At one point in *Heart of Darkness* he makes a close connection between steering and human solidarity when his helmsman is killed:

> Well, don't you see, he had done something, he had steered; for months I had him at my back—a help—an instrument. It was a kind of partnership. He steered for me—I had to look after him, I worried about his deficiencies, and thus a subtle bond had been created, of which I only became aware when it was suddenly broken. (73)

and this is echoed later in his recognition of the necessity of ignorance within the 'safe' society and in his brave lie to Kurtz's fiancée:

[5] Dashiell Hammett, *The Dashiell Hammett Omnibus* (London, 1950), p. 591.

. . . bowing my head before the faith that was in her, before that great
and saving illusion that shone with an unearthly glow in the darkness,
in the triumphant darkness from which I could not have defended
her . . . (108–9).

At the end of each of these two novels the narrator is put forward as an
object for our contemplation, Ishmael floating in a coffin and Marlow
'indistinct and silent, in the pose of a meditating Buddha' (111). In so
contemplating them we see the experience of the novel given shape and
cohesion. This provides an advance upon the pattern of earlier romances
where the hero is torn between opposing value systems, one tending
towards Romantic individualism and the other towards the safety of
rationality and the 'domestic affections', but where there is a clearly
defined retreat to the safe world at the end. This pattern is followed, in
various ways, in Scott's *Waverley* (1814), Mary Shelley's *Frankenstein*
(1818) and Hawthorne's *The Marble Faun* (1860). In such novels it seems
that the readers are offered the possibilities of a learning process which
never materializes. Ishmael and Marlow also go back to the 'safe' society
but not simply as members of it. Rather, they return as explorers who
know more about the darker recesses of human nature than most of the
people with whom they now have to live. As such they are potential
educators.

How far does Nick Carraway (and *The Great Gatsby*) adhere to this
pattern? He begins his journey in a spirit of adventure, relating himself to
those intrepid figures who opened up the new continent:

I was a guide, a pathfinder, an original settler. (10)

and posits himself, true to a recurrent American tradition, as an Adamic
figure starting again in a new world:

I had that familiar conviction that life was beginning over again with
the summer (10).[6]

Chroniclers of the Adamic experience in America, from Melville to
Nathanael West, have insisted that the innocence of that experience must
often be linked to ignorance and certainly Nick has to learn the fallacy of

---

[6] See Walt Whitman in 'Song of Myself':

I, now thirty-seven years old in perfect health begin,
Hoping to cease not till death.

his early statement that 'life is much more successfully looked at from a single window, after all' (10). Enough attention has already been paid to Nick's mistakes and to the increasing complexity of his vision, but his role as a bridge-figure between the dreams of Gatsby, dreams which leave that figure permanently sealed off from humanity:

> A sudden emptiness seemed to flow now from the windows and the great doors, endowing with complete isolation the figure of the host, who stood on the porch, his hand up in a formal gesture of farewell. (62)

and the grim reality of the Valley of Ashes has, perhaps, not been sufficiently accented. In this role Nick seems a spokesman for normality, for that gauge of life's essential rhythms which serves as a pointer to that so necessary sense of human solidarity. Two examples will serve: Nick's early comments on the city suggest a criticism made endlessly by American writers who followed Fitzgerald, that it is a place of masks and elusive identities where nothing is quite what it seems to be. The old man who sells dogs 'bore an absurd resemblance to John D. Rockefeller' (33) and the sex of the dog which Tom buys seems to be a mystery:

> 'Is it a boy or a girl?' she asked delicately.
> 'That dog? That dog's a boy.'
> 'It's a bitch', said Tom decisively (34).

This, of course, links with other confusions in the novel, as when Myrtle mistakes Jordan for Daisy and Gatsby insists that San Francisco is in the Middle West; confusions which, suggests R. W. Stallman, arise partly 'from the confused morality of the epoch'.[7]

Yet even while he is chronicling these Nick can respond much more positively towards the city atmosphere:

> We drove over to Fifth Avenue, warm and soft, almost pastoral, on the summer Sunday afternoon. I wouldn't have been surprised to see a great flock of white sheep turn the corner (34).

Later he expands on this positive feeling:

> I began to like New York, the racy, adventurous feel of it at night, and the satisfaction that the constant flicker of men and women and machines gives to the restless eye (63).

[7] 'Gatsby and the Hole in Time', *op. cit.*, p. 131.

In the same paragraph he is able imaginatively to feel kinship with the lonely young clerks; to feel the milieu as peopled by real beings with real feelings, a position which, for different reasons, is unavailable either to Gatsby or to Tom.

Later, when he rides into New York with Gatsby, he experiences a strange feeling of elation:

> The city seen from the Queensboro Bridge is always the city seen for the first time, in its first wild promise of all the mystery and beauty in the world.
>
> A dead man passed us in a hearse heaped with blooms followed by two carriages with drawn blinds, and by more cheerful carriages for friends. The friends looked out at us with the tragic eyes and short upper lips of south-eastern Europe, and I was glad that the sight of Gatsby's splendid car was included in their sombre holiday. As we crossed Blackwell's Island a limousine passed us, driven by a white chauffeur, in which sat three modish negroes, two bucks and a girl. I laughed aloud as the yolks of their eyeballs rolled toward us in haughty rivalry.
>
> 'Anything can happen now that we've slid over this bridge', I thought; 'anything at all . . .'

Even Gatsby could happen, without any particular wonder (74–5). During my first few readings of the novel I had assumed that Nick saw things in this particular way because of the presence of Gatsby and the consequent influence on Nick's vision of Gatsby's enchanted world. While there is obviously some truth in this there are other (and more important) points to be made about this paragraph. Some commentators have stressed the less than savoury element of racism present here (perhaps to be attributed to Fitzgerald as much as to Nick) and also the paragraph's microcosmic encapsulation of a world of increasing social mobility which provides an ironic endorsement of the ideas which Tom Buchanan has culled from *The Rise of the Coloured Empires*. Moreover, as M. Gidley has acutely pointed out, the image of the socially transformed blacks 'is an extreme version of the transformation of James Gatz, poor boy, into Jay Gatsby, owner of splendid cars, silk shirts, bound books'.[8] Yet beyond all these points another needs to be made. The initial

[8] M. Gidley, 'Notes on F. Scott Fitzgerald and the Passing of the Great Race', *Journal of American Studies*, vol. 7, no. 2 (August, 1973), p. 179.

reference to 'the mystery and beauty of the world' suggests that Nick's vision is akin to Gatsby's, a Platonic one. The language has that sort of resonance. Yet the mystery and beauty is of the world, not beyond it. It is surely no accident that Nick witnesses first the sombreness of death and then the comical vitality of life, so giving rise to a celebration of cycles where life emerges from death. Nick witnesses the inexhaustible variety of life and appreciates it far more than any other character in the novel. Tragedy and comedy are linked indissolubly by both being associated with eyes. The eyes of the Mediterranean immigrants are 'tragic' while the eyes of the blacks make Nick laugh. All this is seen 'without any particular wonder' but accepted for what it is. The immigrants and the blacks do not have to be transformed by the power of a Romantic dream nor do they pose a social threat.

However, Nick's 'education' must still be seen to have large limitations and these come to a head in the concluding few pages of the novel. One signpost of these limitations occurs on the penultimate page when Nick, his bags all packed for his return West, pays a last visit to Gatsby's 'incoherent failure of a house':

> On the white steps an obscene word, scrawled by some boy with a piece of brick, stood out clearly in the moonlight, and I erased it, drawing my shoe raspingly along the stone (187)

This incident was later used by J. D. Salinger in *The Catcher in the Rye* (1951) when Holden goes to see his sister, Phoebe, at her school:

> Somebody'd written 'Fuck you' on the wall. It drove me damn near crazy . . . I was afraid some teacher would catch me rubbing it off and think *I'd* written it. But I rubbed it out anyway, finally.[9]

The link between Nick and Holden is illuminating because Holden's wish to rub them all out, like his wish to see Phoebe going around forever on the carousel, argues a destructive determination to stay within the static world of innocence, a refusal to grow up, to accept the necessities of experience. Despite the progress of his moral education suggested by his dismissal of Jordan, Nick seems to be caught between the Romanticism of Gatsby, imaginative but hopelessly unworkable, and the world of disaster, decay and death signified by Tom's materialism, Wolfsheim's crookedness and the awful emptiness of the Valley of Ashes. It is possible

[9] J. D. Salinger, *The Catcher in the Rye* (New York, 1972), p. 201.

to see Nick, at the end of the novel, as an example of Fitzgerald's dictum that 'the test of a first-rate intelligence is the ability to hold two opposed ideas in the mind . . . and still retain the ability to function' but, as Richard D. Lehan observes:

> The fact that he takes flight at the end of the novel, returning to the Midwest from which he restlessly came in the first place, indicates that he does not really know how to make use of this knowledge and that he will remain torn between a romantic and a realistic disposition of mind.[10]

Instead of Nick being offered as an object for contemplation, the novel ends with him retreating into nostalgia. He links Gatsby's continual sense of wonder with that of the original settlers of America as they became aware of the immense potential of the New World. In *Heart of Darkness* Marlow links his Congo journey to the journey of civilized Romans travelling for the first time to the British Isles, a place at the end of the earth, utterly savage with 'a sea the colour of lead, a sky the colour of smoke', and this has the effect of compressing the history of the earth, of insisting that darkness has never been far away, that savagery is a near cousin to civilization:

> We live in the flicker—may it last as long as the old earth keeps rolling! But darkness was here yesterday (8).

Nick's concluding comments have a similar effect of encapsulating the history of America. One could argue that that history is seen as a story of steady decline from the wonder of the Dutch sailors to the shocking materialism of the 1920s, running pell-mell towards the Great Crash of 1929. Yet perhaps the novel suggests a more complex view, one which sees that the ideal and the real, the vision of Bunyan and the style of Defoe, have always been present in American life, as present in the Puritan doctrine of picayune providence as in the nineteenth-century concept of Manifest Destiny. Such a view of the American inheritance is repeatedly underlined in the novel—in a Carraway history merging the dukes of Buccleuch and a 'wholesale hardware business' (8–9); in the close proximity of *Town Tattle* and *Simon Called Peter*; in Gatsby himself who enters as a magician:

---

[10] F. Scott Fitzgerald and the Craft of Fiction, *op. cit.*, p. 112.

It was one of those rare smiles with a quality of eternal reassurance in it, that you may come across four or five times in life. (54)

and switches rapidly to being only:

. . . an elegant young rough-neck, a year or two over thirty, whose elaborate formality of speech just missed being absurd (54).

Through Nick's narration the novel seems to point to American history as being a microcosm of that duality persistent throughout the history of the world.

However, a strong sense of linear decline in American history still permeates the book. The 1920s must have seemed, to intelligent participants, totally inimical to any sense of wonder at anything. In a deceptively breezy article published in *Atlantic Monthly* in 1920 John F. Carter, Jr remarked about his (and Fitzgerald's) generation:

We have been forced to become realists overnight, instead of idealists, as was our birthright . . . We have seen entire social systems overthrown, and our own called into question. In short, we have seen the inherent beastliness of the human race revealed in an infernal apocalypse.[11]

and, writing two years later, Harold E. Stearns saw the retreat from wonder as a perpetual (and increasing) factor in American life:

In my own day at Harvard the Westerners in my class looked with considerable suspicion upon those who specialized in literature, the classics, or philosophy—a man's education should be science, economics, engineering. Only 'sissies', I was informed, took courses in poetry out in that virile West.[12]

Van Wyck Brooks and other commentators saw the predominant cultural dilemma in America as involving a failure to reconcile the useless extremes of impractical idealism (of which Gatsby may be said to be a

[11] '"These Wild Young People" by One of Them', *op. cit.*, p. 303. Reprinted in Cowley and Cowley (eds), *Fitzgerald and the Jazz Age*, *op. cit.*, p. 49.

[12] Harold E. Stearns, 'The Intellectual Life'. In Harold E. Stearns (ed.), *Civilization in the United States: an Inquiry by Thirty Americans* (New York, 1922), p. 142. Reprinted in Cowley and Cowley, *op. cit.*, p. 80.

representative although he moves beyond such criticism) and 'catch-penny realities'.[13] Certainly the abyss between America's material wealth and spiritual poverty is a crucial issue of the decade.

Gatsby's death seems, in this view, to signal the death of something associated with the past, with innocence, with virtue. Nick tries to articulate this at the end of chapter 6:

> Through all he said, even through his appalling sentimentality, I was reminded of something—an elusive rhythm, a fragment of lost words, that I had heard somewhere a long time ago (118).

The 'elusive rhythm' is that belonging to youth and innocence and dreaming, before the shades of the prison-house begin to close in.

Nick's closing comments seem to ally himself (and us) quite firmly with Gatsby, a sentimental gesture rigorously eschewed elsewhere in the novel. Gary J. Scrimgeour has argued that sentimentality pervades Carraway's view of Gatsby (and Fitzgerald's view of Carraway), that Carraway learns nothing through his experiences and that his defeat is caused by 'his own substitution of dreams for knowledge of self and the world'.[14] The preceding pages of this study should have made it clear that such is not my view but, nevertheless, it seems that although Nick does learn through his experiences he has no way of putting that learning to use. Of course, it needs to be constantly reiterated that Nick is a character in the novel, warts and all, and need not be considered merely as a mouthpiece for Fitzgerald, but his ending retreat to nostalgia indicates perhaps that the alternatives to Gatsby in the novel are too dreadful to contemplate and that Nick in himself cannot find a viable middle way except in retreat. Robert Ornstein, a much more sympathetic critic than Scrimgeour, comes to the same conclusion:

> Yet his return is not a positive rediscovery of the well-springs of American life. Instead it seems a melancholy retreat from the ruined promise of the East, from the empty present to the childhood memory of the past.[15]

[13] Van Wyck Brooks, *Three Essays on America* (New York, 1934), p. 17.

[14] Gary J. Scrimgeour, 'Against *The Great Gatsby*', *Criticism* VIII (Winter, 1966), pp. 75–86. Reprinted in Ernest Lockridge (ed.), *Twentieth Century Interpretations of 'The Great Gatsby'* (Englewood Cliffs, NJ, 1968), p. 79.

[15] Robert Ornstein, 'Scott Fitzgerald's Fable of East and West', *College English* XVIII (1956–7), pp. 139–43. Reprinted in Lockridge, *op. cit.*, p. 59.

Certainly, Nick's return West is not a return to rural innocence from the experience of the city. It is a return to the past but also a return to safety, to a more 'traditional' America away from fantastic scenes by El Greco. Nick's desire for peace and quiet is understandable and does not invalidate his experiences (or his manner of relating them). One might argue that Nick's 'West', like the America to which Lambert Strether returns at the end of Henry James's *The Ambassadors* (1903), is less an actual place than a state of mind resulting from the educative process from which he has emerged. Hence the West might be changed in proportion to the changes which have taken place in Nick's perception of human existence. However, Strether has the advantage that the world he learns from is endlessly various and fully human, very unlike Fitzgerald's waste land. The people who 'teach' Strether—Madame de Vionnet, Maria Gostrey and Chad—while they have their limitations, are fully engaged in the process of living through social interconnections and not, like Gatsby, building a dream securely on a fairy's wing. Strether moves from a view of the world based on polarities of 'good' and 'bad' to a view of human behaviour as an endless series of shades of grey. Given the persistent polarization of the world in *The Great Gatsby* this view is unobtainable to Nick. Therefore the ending of Fitzgerald's novel seems truly bleak. Unlike those of Ishmael and Marlow, Nick's experiences offer little hope of a middle ground in human solidarity because his human world is a thinner, more corrupt place, constantly threatening to topple over into complete dissolution. Despite his relationships Nick remains as solitary at the end of his story as at the beginning. By the end he seems closer to Huckleberry Finn than to the heroes of Melville and Conrad, driven by the mendacity of the world to 'light out' for territories whose very existence is in doubt. If Nick is to be seen as an educator, then the lesson he has to teach is, indeed, a dark one.

Select Bibliography

(Place of publication, New York, except where otherwise specified)

Collections

Kenneth E. Eble (ed.), *F. Scott Fitzgerald* (1973).

Frederick J. Hoffman (ed.), *'The Great Gatsby': a Study* (1962).

Alfred Kazin (ed.), *F. Scott Fitzgerald: the Man and his Work* (1951).

Ernest Lockridge (ed.), *Twentieth Century Interpretations of 'The Great Gatsby'* (Englewood Cliffs, NJ, 1968).

Arthur Mizener (ed.), *F. Scott Fitzgerald: a Collection of Critical Essays* (Englewood Cliffs, NJ, 1963).

Books and Articles

Matthew J. Bruccoli, *Apparatus for F. Scott Fitzgerald's 'The Great Gatsby'* (Columbia, South Carolina, 1974).

John F. Callahan, *The Illusions of a Nation* (Urbana, 1972).

Kenneth Eble, 'The Craft of Revision: *The Great Gatsby*', *American Literature* XXXVI (1964–5), pp.315–26. Reprinted in Eble, *op. cit.*

William A. Fahey, *F. Scott Fitzgerald and the American Dream* (1973).

Sheilah Graham, *College of One* (1967).

Richard D. Lehan, *F. Scott Fitzgerald and the Craft of Fiction* (Carbondale and Edwardsville, 1966).

James E. Miller, Jr, *F. Scott Fitzgerald: his Art and his Technique* (1964).

Arthur Mizener, *The Far Side of Paradise* (Boston, 1951).

Sergio Perosa, *The Art of F. Scott Fitzgerald* (Ann Arbor, 1965).

Henry Dan Piper, *F. Scott Fitzgerald: a Critical Portrait* (1965).

Robert Sklar, *F. Scott Fitzgerald: the Last Laocoön* (1967).

R. W. Stallman, *The Houses that James Built* (East Lansing, 1961).

Milton R. Stern, *The Golden Moment* (Urbana, 1970).

Andrew Turnbull, *Scott Fitzgerald* (1962).

Index